OKLAHOMA **TRACKMAKER** SERIES

OKLAHOMA **TRACKMAKER** SERIES

The Cart That Changed the World

Sylvan N. Goldman

THE CART THAT CHANGED THE WORLD

The Career of *SYLVAN N. GOLDMAN*

By
Terry P. Wilson

Odie B. Faulk, Series Editor

Published for the Oklahoma Heritage Association
by the University of Oklahoma Press

Library of Congress Cataloging in Publication Data
Wilson, Terry P.   1941–
   The cart that changed the world.

   (Oklahoma trackmaker series)
   "Outgrowth of a dissertation written at Oklahoma State University."
   Bibliography: p. 245.
   Includes index.
   1. Goldman, Sylvan Nathan, 1898– 2. Supermarkets—United States. 3. Businessmen—United States—Biography. 4. Inventors—United States—Biography. I. Title. II. Series.
HF5469.W55   381 [B]   78–58074

For my mother and father

Preface

Less than one hundred years ago hardy pioneers rushed into Oklahoma to create instant cities, clear the land, and plant crops. When teachers of Oklahoma history tell their students about this era, they normally concentrate on the farmers and ranchers who raced for land, giving little attention to the pioneer merchants of the territory and state. One such merchant, Sylvan N. Goldman, was the son of a pioneer who made that rush. His life, from his birth in the Indian Territory in 1898 to the present, spans almost the entirety of the state's modern history. Unfortunately, he has not chosen to write an autobiography. Had he done so, his recollections would constitute a valuable record of the economic and social history of much of the state, for he has had an astonishing business career and long years of civic and cultural involvement. Instead Goldman has chosen to let his deeds speak for themselves. Doubtless he agrees with Henry Havelock Ellis, who once commented that "every artist writes his autobiography in his works."

Yet a biography of Sylvan N. Goldman is needed, for a knowledge of his life and contributions can add to our understanding of how modern Oklahoma was built. He is a living symbol of the forty-sixth state's frontier heritage and of its opportunities for men of vision with a willingness to work. In addition, Goldman stands almost alone among America's twentieth-century pioneers as a developer of the business frontier of the nation. Through his commercial innovations, products of his independent thinking, he changed the buying habits of all Americans and wrought a commercial revolution that has spread around the world. Then, as his wealth increased, he became noted for his many civic and philanthropic endeavors. Today, at a time when most men his age have long since retired, he continues to innovate, to work, and to give.

"The history of the world is but the biography of great men," Thomas Carlyle once stated. Benjamin Disraeli echoed that same truth when he commented, "Read no history: nothing but biography, for that is life without theory." This book is a substitute for the autobiography Goldman has declined to write. To read the story of his continuing career is to see the opportunity that the United States has represented during the first three-quarters of this century.

Writing in the *New York Times* of October 4, 1975, Lawrence Van Gelder recognized this extraordinary individual, stating, "There breathes hardly any American, young or old" who is not indebted to Sylvan N. Goldman of Oklahoma City. "Goldman," Van Gelder wrote, "is a unique individual who created an invention that ranks high among contributions to life around the world." He was referring to Goldman's invention of the supermarket shopping cart and later the airport luggage cart, without which "life would not be the same."

In interviewing Goldman for this story, Van Gelder said he had been assigned to write an article on "the most important item for public use on four wheels, second only to the automobile." Van Gelder wrote:

> Everybody knows about Henry Ford and the Wright Brothers. But what about Sylvan N. Goldman? Despite his innovations he lives in virtual anonymity. No postage stamp

bears his likeness; no awesome monument honors his creation.

From its humble Depression-era beginning in a carpentry shop in Oklahoma City in 1937, the shopping cart and later the luggage cart—like the automobile—have become big business.

In their ubiquitous but unremarkable way, they have rolled along with American and world social history in the latter two-thirds of the twentieth century—rising out of the Depression; meeting the post-War baby boom with the folding baby seat; joining the exodus to the suburbs and, predictably, exportation to every corner of the world.

Looking back on it all, Mr. Goldman, a prominent Oklahoman whose interests are now concentrated in real estate, spoke with a mixture of pride and modesty about the invention that changed life in America and around the world. "It made a world of difference," he said, "but if it hadn't been me somebody else would have invented it."

Patrick Henry, in a speech to the Virginia Convention in 1775, said, "I have but one lamp by which my feet are guided and that is the lamp of experience." Sylvan N. Goldman was educated in the same school. Early in life he lighted that lamp and used it to guide his feet unerringly up the road to success. The light from that lamp reveals an extraordinary man living in an extraordinary period who made extraordinary contributions to humanity.

No author writes in a vacuum; inspiration, guidance, and encouragement are necessary ingredients. I was fortunate in having all of these from Sylvan N. Goldman, who gave generously of his time, made available his corporate and personal records, and added to the project his zestful enthusiasm for life. In addition, members of Goldman Enterprises were helpful in offering information, interest, and insight. I am also grateful to the Oklahoma Heritage Association and its staff for the assistance given me there.

The Cart That Changed the World

This work is the outgrowth of a dissertation written at Oklahoma State University, and to my major adviser, Joseph A. Stout, Jr., I express my sincere and heartfelt thanks. Odie B. Faulk, editor of the Trackmaker Series, helped in preparing the final draft, and to him I am grateful. Finally, I thank the editorial staff of the University of Oklahoma Press for the deft touches they have added. Without the assistance of all these persons, I would not have been able to complete this task.

TERRY P. WILSON

University of California, Berkeley

Contents

Illustrations

The Cart That Changed the World

Young Sylvan Goldman, seated by his mother, Hortense, his father, Michael, and older brother, Alfred, standing. (Goldman Collection)

1. *From Ardmore to the Argonne*

On January 11, 1977, morning and afternoon newspapers across the United States carried an advertisement for a new magazine-format television series called "Who's Who." In bold letters the advertisement stated that viewers that evening would get "an inside look at the man who has affected the lives of every American shopper." The accompanying picture was a photograph of Sylvan N. Goldman.

That evening on CBS Television, Charles Kuralt was the host of a segment entitled "Shopping Cart Man." Kuralt opened by saying: "Sylvan N. Goldman is an important man. . . . When I heard about him I knew I had to meet him. . . . Sylvan N. Goldman owns land and banks and things. But it's not what he does; it's what he did. What he did was—invent the shopping cart." Kuralt continued:

> Before we learn to walk, or talk these days, we learn which package contains the Crackerjacks and which holds merely pickles. If there were no shopping carts, nothing to roll our children and our Campbell's soup around the store in, what would become of us? There might never have been a supermarket. There might never have been a giant economy-sized Kellogg's Rice Krispies. It boggles the mind.

Kuralt was pointing out that this invention by an innovative Oklahoma City merchant changed the face of America. It made possible the mass merchandising of food. It changed the shopping and social patterns of all Americans and spread around the world to influence a large percentage of the world's buying and merchandising habits.

Unfortunately, however, Charles Kuralt was concentrating on only one aspect of Sylvan N. Goldman's life and contributions. Had he become more knowledgeable about this remarkable and extraordinary Oklahoman, Kuralt could have spoken about Goldman's contributions to the business world, as well as the more subtle monuments he has left in the form of philanthropic contributions to more than a score of worthwhile charities.

The pioneering spirit was part of Goldman's heritage. His father, Michael Goldman, earlier had demonstrated initiative and ambition. Born in the tiny Baltic state of Latvia, young Michael Goldman immigrated in 1880 to Baltimore, Maryland. An uncle, the owner of a small dry-goods store in that city, had asked his brother to send a son to the United States to work in the establishment. Arriving in Baltimore, young Michael divided his time between the dry-goods store and a nearby school. Soon after achieving a working knowledge of the English language and of the customs of his new country, he made a decision that was to have a great effect on his own future and on that of his descendants. He decided to move West.[1]

Michael's decision came as a result of the opening of part of the Indian Territory, the Unassigned Lands, to settlement. President Benjamin Harrison proclaimed that on April 22, 1889, approximately two million acres would be opened to homesteading. Government planners knew that Americans wanted more free or inexpensive land than was available in Oklahoma Territory, and they decided to allow everyone interested to "run" for quarter-section homesteads or town lots. Young Goldman decided to make the run.

On the appointed day he entered Oklahoma riding in the wagon of a friendly family. Like thousands of other Boomers, he was unable to establish a claim that day. He stayed briefly in the "instant town" Oklahoma City and then journeyed to Ardmore, in the south-central portion of the territory. There he used his two hundred dollars in savings to purchase a 160-acre tract. Because he knew so little about farming, however, he soon moved across the border into Texas, where at Gainesville he obtained a job with the Kahn Brothers Wholesale Groceries, Produce and Dry Goods Company. It was an association that was to prove far more enduring than he or his employers perhaps realized.

The Kahns had emigrated in the early 1880's from Alsace-Lorraine, then part of the German Empire, and settled in Gainesville. After starting a thriving wholesale enterprise in Gainesville, the brothers began bringing relatives from Europe to work in their company. Among those who arrived in this manner were two nephews, Samuel and Henry Dreyfus, and later their sister Hortense. Hortense was fifteen and the oldest girl in the large family. While her brothers (three more were to arrive soon) learned the intricacies of their uncles' business affairs, she tried to fathom the folkways of the American West. After his arrival Michael Goldman began courting her. The two were married in the spring of 1894.

The following year the young couple moved to Davis, in the Indian Territory, where Goldman became manager of a failing general store that the Kahns had taken over. Struggling to make the business a success, he paused on June 7, 1895, to celebrate the birth of his first child, Alfred Dreyfus Goldman. Some time later the store, operating profitably under Goldman's management, was sold, and the family moved to Ardmore. There he nursed yet another ailing store to health. Except for a two-year interval (1902 to 1904), when the family lived in Dougherty (an engine stop on the Santa Fe Railroad near Sulphur, Indian Territory), Goldman operated the general store in Ardmore and the one in Dougherty until 1913.[2]

On page 3 of the *Daily Ardmoreite* of November 15, 1898, was a brief announcement: "Born: This morning to Mr. and Mrs. Mike Goldman, a son."[3] The second son was named Sylvan Nathan Goldman.

Ardmore was a young, energetic frontier town. When the first white men settled the area, the Chickasaw Indian Nation occupied much of the region under the terms of a federal treaty. The 700 Ranch, operated by a succession of owners beginning about 1880, provided the future townsite with its first buildings, which served as a convenient stopping place for deputy marshals, including Heck Thomas and Bill Tilghman, who strove to curtail the lawlessness of the Indian Territory. Bill Dalton, leader of the notorious Dalton Gang, was killed near Ardmore in 1892. According to the local newspapers, the town was plagued by unruly elements until its incorporation in December, 1899.[4]

With the extension of the Gulf, Colorado and Santa Fe Railroad from Gainesville north through the Chickasaw lands came construction of the actual community of Ardmore. A Texas contractor, George B. Douglas, realized the importance of the site as a rail depot and moved his family to the 700 Ranch early in 1886. By the end of February he had readied not only a log cabin for his personal use but also a stockade and a series of sheds for commercial use. On July 28, 1887, the first train arrived at the new depot, which for years was a converted boxcar, and deposited a shipment of building materials. These were quickly

Hortense Goldman with son Sylvan, photograph taken at Ardmore, Indian Territory. (Goldman Collection)

put to use because by 1890 the rail connections had attracted two thousand settlers. That same year the growth of the village was further stimulated when it was chosen as the site for a United States district court. Its underlying economic base, however, was cotton ginning and sales in southern Oklahoma.[5]

The Goldmans discovered an active Jewish community in Ardmore. One of the town's first retail establishments, the widely known Iron Store (named for its corrugated-iron construction) was opened in 1888 by two Jewish Texans, Max Munzeheimer and Samuel Daube. An employee of the store, Max Westheimer, soon joined Frank Wymore in opening the Blue Front Store, which later was named Westheimer and Daube after David Daube purchased Wymore's interest. The Jewish community was also active in the town's religious life. In 1898, Temple Emeth was organized as a Reform congregation. Meeting first in private homes and public halls, the congregation later purchased the First Christian Church for use as a temple. Thirteen-year-old Sylvan Goldman underwent his bar mitzvah there in 1912.[6]

Growing up Jewish in Oklahoma was an anomalous experience. Most of the time young Goldman's boyhood was like that of any other Ardmore youth. He occasionally was made aware of his ethnic heritage, however. One incident, which occurred when he was in his early teens, gave Goldman an insight into the gentile majority's attitude toward its Jewish neighbors. Walking home from school with two Protestant classmates, he was asked why the Jews did not worship Jesus Christ as Christians did. Goldman, one of only three Jewish children in Ardmore's first ward school, explained that the first of the Ten Commandments in the Book of Exodus in the Bible said, "Thou shalt have no other gods before me."

His reply failed to satisfy the other boys, who then wanted to know why the Jews worshiped on Saturdays instead of Sundays. This question stumped Goldman. Intrigued, he asked his father across the dinner table that evening to unravel the Sabbath puzzle. The elder Goldman offered a biblical reference from the fourth commandment by way of explanation: "For in six days the Lord made heaven and earth, the sea and all that in them is, and rested the seventh day: wherefore the Lord blessed the sabbath day and hallowed it." The next morning, following his father's instructions, Goldman quoted the scripture and challenged his gentile friends to count the days of the week to prove that Saturday, the seventh day, was indeed a legitimate time to worship.[7]

Goldman received all of his eight years of formal education in Ardmore's public schools. The brevity of his tenure in the classroom in no way reflected lack of concern for learning or academic attendance. School was an enjoyable experience for him, and he was an exceptionally attentive student. A former schoolteacher, Mrs. Grace Carr, described him as "a very ambitious child with a good mind."[8] Goldman was able to make use of his favorite subject, mathematics, at an early age. In addition to doing the usual chores assigned youngsters in those days, he helped his father in the dry-goods store after school. Surprisingly, in view of his later success as a businessman, Goldman had no particular liking for the store. In fact, he has recalled that if the working experience had any effect on his later career it was to ensure that his future business endeavors would be confined to fields other than dry goods.

Goldman's entry into the business world full time came rather abruptly. In 1913 his father sold the family store, and the Goldmans moved to Tulsa. There Mrs. Goldman's five brothers, Samuel, Henry, Gabe, Asher, and Morris Dreyfus, who had moved from Gainesville, were operating a wholesale grocery and produce business that was prospering as a result of the oil boom in that region of the state. At the age of fifteen Goldman began working at his uncles' branch store in Sapulpa, an oil-field community and division point of the Santa Fe Railroad that required a separate warehouse and office because of the poor, often impassable roads that linked it with Tulsa. Apparently the grocery, fruit, and vegetable business was more attractive to Goldman than was dry goods, for he was to make groceries and produce his major concerns for the next forty-five years, except for one important interruption.

Life in Sapulpa was pleasant enough. Samuel Dreyfus, who managed the branch store taught his nephew the fundamentals of the wholesale grocery business. Goldman worked as a shipping clerk and also sold to restaurants the fresh fruits and vegetables distributed by Dreyfus Brothers, Wholesalers.[9] Not all of Goldman's time was spent at work. He found time to acquire many friends. One of them, Harold N. Reed, later described him as "a typical, happy-go-lucky American."[10]

In 1917, after four years in Sapulpa, Goldman joined hundreds of thousands of others across the nation in their generation's great adventure, World War I. News of the war in Europe had filled the pages of Oklahoma newspapers since 1914. Despite the reelection in 1916 of Woodrow Wilson, who campaigned on the slogan "He kept us out of war," many Americans believed and some ardently hoped that the United States would enter the conflict. Because of close cultural ties with England, Allied propaganda, and unrestricted submarine warfare, most Americans viewed Kaiser Wilhelm and the Central Powers as their natural enemies. In Tulsa the Chamber of Commerce decided to ready the community for the coming conflict by raising a military unit composed of local citizens. An organizational meeting was held in February, 1917, to discuss the exciting project. By the time Congress declared war on April 6, two companies had been formed and were accepting enlistments.[11] A recruiting tent was set up at the corner of Fourth and Main Streets.

On April 25, 1917, Goldman and two Sapulpa friends went to Tulsa to enlist. Harold N. Reed and Goldman added their names to Company A, First Battalion, Oklahoma Engineers; the other member of the trio joined an ambulance company that was also accepting volunteers. Reed, who was twenty-one, met the minimum-age requirement, but Goldman had to stretch his age by eighteen months. The two joined a growing company impatiently awaiting word from the War Department about mobilization and training. All these volunteers were Oklahomans with a wide cross-section of occupations including oil-field workers, farmers, and college students. Many of the students were from Henry Kendall College (now the University of Tulsa), where a few had majored in civil engineering. They were to get a chance to put that education to practical use in France.[12]

After a hurried visit to the state capital the new unit received authorization to move onto the property of an old National Guard company of engineers in Tulsa. At the same time the company adopted the traditional National Guard table of organization. It was authorized to have a complement of commissioned personnel consisting of a captain, two first lieutenants, and one second lieutenant. Immediately after the declaration of war, Van T. Moon received a commission as captain and company commander. His first lieutenants were Forrest R. Hughes and Jack Singleton, while Gordon T. Granger completed the list of officers as second lieutenant. All four men remained in those capacities for the duration of the war. Late in April the company, under its new officers, was officially mustered into federal service and began regular drilling. Neither the engineers nor the ambulance company had barracks until August 5, when the Tulsa fairgrounds became Camp Sinclair. Two weeks later came orders finally for departure to training areas.[13]

Eighteen hours by rail brought the eager recruits to Camp

Bowie, outside Fort Worth, Texas. Disappointment and disillusionment quickly followed. The Tulsans learned that the regular army had definite ideas about readying raw recruits for action. News of the delay of nearly a year before reaching the field of combat also disheartened the Oklahomans. Even the most eager recruit must have felt a dampening of enthusiasm that first night at Bowie. A driving rain had turned the camp into a quagmire of foot-deep mud. Following a hasty meal of canned corned beef, beans, and hardtack, the men retired to the relative comfort of an empty warehouse. The next day companies of engineers from Ardmore and Oklahoma City joined the Tulsans to form, respectively, E and F companies of the Second Battalion, 111th Engineers. Captain Moon's men made up D Company. Three Texas companies formed the First Battalion of the regiment, which was assigned to the Thirty-sixth Division.

The army seemed to be determined that these Texas and Oklahoma engineers would be combat-ready as soon as possible. Ignoring the usual grumbling by new soldiers, experienced trainers led them through practical engineering problems in addition to the usual regimen of infantry training. Naturally, certain specialized positions had to be filled, and young Goldman was named mess sergeant. Despite his youth (his true age being unknown to those making the selection) the choice was an obvious one. His experience in the wholesale business had given him considerable knowledge in judging the quality and estimating the uses of groceries on a large scale. Goldman tackled the myriad tasks of preparing food for two hundred men under all kinds of conditions with the good humor and determination that characterized his later business activities. Before long D Company was praising the improved quality of its meals.

The man responsible was "Sergeant Goldie," an inevitable nickname in an army enamored of acronyms and abbreviations.[14]

Nearby Fort Worth offered some diversions from the discipline of Camp Bowie. Unfortunately, the increasing numbers of trainees stationed at the post posed a problem common to most cities and towns close to military facilities: too many uniformed men on the streets looking for entertainment and finding only others like themselves. Goldman and his cooks had less time than other soldiers to explore the enticements of the Texas city. After cleaning up after the evening meal, the mess sergeant immediately began planning and preparing for the next morning's breakfast, much to the displeasure of the kitchen staff.

All the members of the Oklahoma company went home on furlough at least once during those months at Bowie. Goldman's visit to Tulsa included a pointed inquiry by his mother about the wisdom of his haste in enlisting. The young sergeant made lengthy explanations to prevent his mother from taking the drastic action of effecting his discharge from the army because of his age. Goldman told her that such a move would not be effective; he would simply re-enlist elsewhere. Mrs. Goldman gave in and reluctantly waved her son good-by as he left for camp.[15]

The regiment endured the winter of 1917–18, hoping for orders that would send it to France. Spring and early summer found the engineers still constructing railroads for the post's use and becoming increasingly restive under army discipline. The men doubtless would have approved the rueful wit of a fellow doughboy stationed at another camp. That impatient trooper, seeing a sign posted by a traveling evangelist, "Where Will You Spend Eternity?" had scrawled beneath it, "At Camp McClellan."[16] The summer was half gone before the men of the 111th received orders sending them to France. On July 7 the regiment boarded a train for the East Coast. Once in motion the army wasted little time processing the troops at Camp Mills, on Long Island, New York, to send them across the Atlantic. Only eleven days elapsed from the time they left Camp Bowie until they and their equipment were aboard the freighter U.S.S. *Antigone* and steaming out of New York harbor.

It would probably be impossible to find a veteran of World War I with fond memories of the troopship that carried him and his comrades across the Atlantic. After some fumbling starts the navy had solved the basic problems of overcrowded harbor facilities, inexperience in handling the unprecedented numbers of men and matériel, and the constant hazard of U-boat attack. Arrivals and departures had been streamlined; ships had been converted for transport duties, and the vessels had been painted in alternating black, white, and gray stripes, ostensibly to confuse enemy submarines by breaking up the ships' normal silhouettes. For the troops on these ships, however, the voyage was miserable.

Efficiency in convoying troops did not include planning for the comfort of the human cargo. Bunks were stacked in four tiers and placed so close together that the men had to move sideways, crablike, between the rows. Added to the crowded conditions was the stifling atmosphere below decks. The miserable accommodations caused Goldman to seek an alternative. In an out-of-the-way spot on deck he discovered in the mass of equipment a large coil of thick rope. It served as a circular bunk, complete with fresh air (and occasional rain). Even this retreat failed to protect him from the almost universal shipboard disorder, seasickness. The troops from the rolling plains of the Southwest could not cope with the rolling decks of the *Antigone*; soon they had renamed the vessel the "Agony."

After an otherwise uneventful twelve-day crossing, the men gladly disembarked at the port of Brest on the extreme west coast of France.[17] Stumbling down the gangplanks onto French soil under a drizzling sky, many still feeling the ill effects of the voyage, they shouldered full packs and marched into the countryside. In their discomfort some probably recalled, ironically, the postcards they had addressed in New York two weeks earlier. Provided by the Red Cross, these cards carried a printed message: "The ship on which I sailed has arrived safely overseas." These communications, sent on receipt of a cable confirming the ship's successful crossing of the Atlantic, may have described the condition of the ship, but hardly the weakened state of its passengers.

Perhaps the satisfaction at having solid, unmoving ground beneath their feet would have been greater if the muddy roads had been less slippery.[18] After a march of several hours the men believed that they had reached their destination. They came to several low-lying structures that looked like military barracks built alongside the road. Their guess that the buildings were designed for that purpose was correct; however, the doughboys were not to be the occupants. German prisoners of war were confined in the buildings, while the Americans marched to an open field where they rapidly set up pup tents to form a temporary bivouac.

Goldman and his tentmate took elaborate precautions against dampness. They spread their raincoats on the muddy ground and laid overcoats on top of them to make a dry spot on which to sleep. The next morning the two awakened, soaked to the skin though they had slept fully clothed. Luckily the regiment repacked its gear after another wet night and journeyed by rail to Bar-sur-Aube in De la Aube.

Company D was billeted in the village Argançon. Goldman installed his kitchen near some barns where several soldiers were staying. He and one of the cooks were lucky to rent a room in a nearby farmhouse. During the next month the officers and men drilled hard, familiarizing themselves with French techniques of construction and other technical aspects of the duty they soon would face. Ordinarily new units were assigned to quiet sectors of the front for a few weeks' recuperation from their trips aboard the troopships. This orientation process was denied the 111th, for the regiment unexpectedly was selected to be corps engineers for the First Army Corps. On September 10 the regiment entrained for the front and some of the heaviest American action in the war.[19]

When the United States entered the conflict in 1917, fighting on the Western Front had stagnated into dull, deadly trench warfare. The Germans had lost their chance to seize Paris in 1914, but French and English attempts to push them back in subsequent years had cost more lives than the regained real estate warranted. President Woodrow Wilson, expecting the initial American contribution to the war to be confined to supplying arms and munitions, was dismayed to discover the true status of the Allied position. The German army's chances appeared alarmingly good when, in the spring of 1918, American troops began massing in numbers sufficient to make themselves felt. Because of the collapse of Russia in December, 1917, the kaiser could transfer a sufficient number of soldiers westward to have an advantage of one hundred thousand men over the British and French on the Western Front. Moreover, the morale of the Allied armies was debatable.

General weariness with the war and lengthening casualty lists had already produced mutinies that were barely quelled among the French front-line men, who were disgusted and angered by their staff officers' ineptitude. While matters had not reached this low state among British troops, no one could testify to the continued reliability of the haggard Tommies.

Adding to the problems of Allied officers was the thorny issue of unified military operations. A renewed German offensive in March, 1918, spurred a long-overdue decision to place all Allied armies under one supreme commander. French Marshal Ferdinand Foch got the job and along with it the sensitive problem of where and how to use the American doughboys. The British earlier had suggested shipping American recruits to Great Britain for training and then sending them to the front under British officers. To General John J. Pershing, commander-in-chief of the American Expeditionary Force, this idea was as unthinkable as the French plan to attach small units of the AEF to existing French units. Pershing insisted on a separate American army with a defined sector of the front as its responsibility—he had not crossed the Atlantic to command a replacement center for the Allies. His eyes were focused on the Saint-Mihiel salient, one of three bulges poking into France along the line of trenches that stretched irregularly from the Belgian coast on the North Sea across parts of three countries to Switzerland. Pershing proposed breaking the salient and driving north to seize Metz, an important railroad and mining center. Foch objected to the plan, but Pershing was adamant about maintaining an individual American army. Reluctantly Foch approved the Saint-Mihiel offensive, but he vetoed the Metz drive, insisting that the bulk of Pershing's forces must be transferred to the Argonne immediately after they cracked the salient.[20]

The 111th Engineers arrived at Frovard, near Nancy, on the east flank of the Saint-Mihiel salient, during the second week of September, 1918. They arrived by train and spent the next two months continuously at the front. As a detached unit they were sent where they were most needed, which usually was the place of heaviest action. Goldman's responsibility for feeding the engineers included drawing rations from the huge food stockpiles behind the American advance, a task that involved driving horse-drawn wagons on nocturnal journeys to obtain supplies.[21] Getting supplies was relatively simple for units that were parts of regular formations. However, Goldman and his kitchen crew encountered many obstacles. The officers in charge of the provisions, who were attached to another division, refused Goldman's requests for food, for the AEF had provided no written authorizations for ration issues for the detached engineer. The young Oklahoman was quickly forced to develop that talent for which the American military became famous—scrounging.

Goldman "requisitioned" the necessary items by stratagem. Each night he selected a crew of volunteers, loaded them on wagons, and set off for the rear in search of food. When they sighted a supply depot, the foraging team went into action. Goldman engaged the attention of the guards while his volunteers hastily loaded supplies. This tactic worked smoothly, since the rear areas were not allowed to burn lights for fear of air attack, and the supply depots were not heavily guarded.

Members of the 111th later recalled these expeditions gleefully and praised the excellent meals they enjoyed as a result of their sergeant's ingenuity.[22] On one occasion the expedition to gather food proved dangerous. Goldman and a transportation company teamster were driving a team of horses one night when the dreaded signal warning of a poison-gas barrage was sounded. The two men lost no time reaching for their gas masks, ordinarily a quick maneuver, for regulations required each soldier to wear his mask around his neck at all times. Unfortunately, the teamster had laid his mask on the wagon seat, and Goldman did not realize that the man could not find it at once; it was on the floorboard where it had been jounced by the bad roads. Goldman put on his mask and jumped off the wagon to help place gas masks on the horses. The teamster finally found his mask. He put it on and helped Goldman quiet the horses. But during the time he was looking for the mask, the deadly gas entered his respiratory system, and he later died from the effects of it.[23]

Other nighttime excursions also proved dangerous. During the drive in the Meuse Argonne, enemy reconnaissance flights made travel hazardous even by night. The men were forbidden to show any lights for fear of triggering German artillery or air bombardment. On one of Goldman's food-procurement trips sparks from a backfiring truck were enough to provide a memorable experience. Realizing the peril of staying with the vehicle as bombs from an airplane began bursting around them, Goldman and four others leaped from the truck and raced for a less-exposed position. A short distance from the road they discovered a small cave. They were about to enter it, when voices from inside indicated that it was already packed with doughboys. The foraging party immediately demonstrated their aptitude for improvising. They dropped to the ground and crawled into the cave between the legs of the standing soldiers. All five of them survived the bombing.

Captain Moon, the company commander, in a letter that

he wrote home to Tulsa, described the work that his engineers were doing. They were repairing and maintaining roads and bridges vital to the flow of munitions and provisions to the doughboys on the front lines. "We were not close enough to get a shot at the Hun," Moon said, "but we were close enough to get his shellfire." [24]

After Saint-Mihiel the engineers of the 111th started a long march to the Argonne Forest, the scene of the next offensive. Walking by night and sleeping by day, the company moved more than eighty miles on a course paralleling the front. On the morning of September 26, 1918, when the infantry troops went over the top, Company D followed three hundred yards behind. In a repeat of their experience at Saint-Mihiel, the engineers performed their construction chores to the accompaniment of regular artillery shelling and bombing by planes on moonlit nights. These attacks continued during a lull in the fighting before the last phase of the Argonne campaign began on October 31.

Besides the intermittent annoyance of German artillery, the men's chief complaint was boredom. Goldman knew the tedium of the trenches, which on one occasion inspired an episode he remembered well. Tobacco was among the supplies shipped from home to bolster morale. In battle zones it was used more for chewing then for smoking, because a lighted cigarette often attracted the attention of enemy pilots. To ease the tension of waiting, Goldman tried some of the tobacco, although he admitted to "more spitting than chewing." Any chance that the young Oklahoman might have carried the habit home was abruptly destroyed when a shell concussion knocked him to the ground, causing him to swallow the tobacco. Goldman later recalled, "That was the end of me and chewing tobacco." [25]

During the first ten days of November the men of the

111th witnessed a renewal of the Argonne—Meuse River battle. Company D was closely involved in the action, repairing roads and bridges for the infantry and artillery. The capture of a German fieldpiece and its ammunition excited some of the Oklahomans' imaginations; they turned the gun around and began shelling in the direction of the enemy. The engineers decided to stick to their own specialties when a courier rushed back to find out who was lobbing shells at the American troops from the rear. On November 10 the company was ordered to pull back and march to Saint-Mihiel for the long-anticipated drive on Metz. At eleven o'clock the next morning, however, came confirmation of an earlier rumor that an armistice had been signed. That night the worn-out engineers reached the forest near Apremont and stopped for a five-day rest. The first night was a memorable one. The celebrating soliders seemed to be trying to fire all their excess ammunition, commemorating the war's end.

When the fighting ceased, the engineers' work was just beginning. Relieved of duty as corps engineers, they started their last long march. On November 29, Company D completed a 180-mile hike to the village of Charrey in Yonne Department. For the next six months the Oklahomans labored at a quarry, extracting materials to rebuild French roads damaged in the war. To maintain morale, the company issued a small number of passes every two weeks. Goldman received a pass, and he took advantage of the opportunity to visit Nice. The entire city, with the exception of one hotel, had been reserved for AEF personnel. A famous resort center in peacetime, Nice, with its music, dancing and wine, reflected the postwar euphoria.

The brief respite from the drudgery at Charrey failed to dissipate the growing eagerness of Goldman and his companions to return home. After a series of depressing false rumors, the 111th Regiment finally received orders to entrain for Le Mans, where it would prepare for the voyage home. On May 20 the engineers boarded the U.S.S. *Great Northern* at Brest. They steamed into Hoboken, New Jersey, harbor six days later.

Goldman went across the Hudson River to Manhattan to enjoy some entertainment before heading home, and it was there that he first saw Will Rogers, who was appearing in the Ziegfeld Follies.

As Hamlet philosophized to Horatio in the last scene of Shakespeare's great drama, "There's a divinity that shapes our ends, rough-hew them how we will." More than fifty years later Goldman wrote, "I remember when I returned from France at the end of World War I, I had the opportunity to see Will Rogers in the Ziegfeld Follies in New York. Standing in the spotlight on the huge stage, twirling his lariat, the Oolagah, Oklahoma, cowboy star eased the memories of the war in the mind of a weary twenty-one-year-old Oklahoma soldier." The effect of that night of entertainment and the part it ultimately played in the life of young Sergeant Goldie will be detailed later.

When Goldman and his fellow soliders reached Tulsa at last, they found the city prepared for their return. Thousands cheered the engineers as they marched under a specially constructed arch of triumph erected on Main Street with funds raised by the American Legion. Following this enthusiastic welcome, the company traveled on to Camp Bowie, Texas, to be mustered out of service on June 20, 1919. The unit had compiled an impressive record. Three times the men were cited in dispatches, once by General Pershing.

Today, the surviving members of Company D meet annually to recall the hectic events and adventures of World War I. Nostalgia reigns supreme at these gatherings. Those events, terrible in the happening, assume a lighter tone with the mellowing years. Goldman rarely misses the reunions and the chance to renew the rare comradeship of men who have known war together. In unison with the other survivors, he expresses no regret at the experience. He sums up his feelings by saying, "I think it [the war] was the best thing that ever happened to me, since I came back alive." If the youth who enlisted on a whim had learned a lesson from the carnage of the Western Front, it was that life was inestimably worth living.

2. A Prosperous Decade

Upon returning home, young Sylvan Goldman reflected on the freedoms for which the war had been fought. Among these he found dearest was freedom of opportunity. This he savored perhaps because he had only an eighth-grade education in the Ardmore public schools, perhaps because of an inflexibly deep and abiding family relationship, or perhaps for other, inborn reasons. The abiding philosophy of his mother has always strengthened him. She quietly impressed on him her belief that human talent is a precious and rare gift. "We gain strength from our faith that only free men can develop their potential to the full," she often emphasized. So freedom of opportunity was the key, the overriding force, that would dominate almost six decades of Goldman's business enterprises.

But there was more, so much more that is undocumented, to say about Goldman. What kind of a man was he, really? What made the young man tick? He carried within him a peculiar form of "fear" that can best be described as courage. He accepted his unceasing struggle between himself and circumstances and the condition of the times. He knew that the feelings gave him power and led to knowledge and understanding. Guiding his every activity were Plato's words: "The beginning is the most important part of the work." For Goldman the beginning of every venture was the same: "Succeed!"

In reviewing the career of a man of myriad successes there are questions to be asked but really never answered: What gives him the force? The courage? The guts? In Goldman pride and self-interest always came first. He had a love of bigness and a reckless, forge-ahead ambition. He believed that each man makes his own world and is at the center of it. Goldman's career reflected this combination of imagination, initiative, enthusiasm, inspiration, and originality. He believed in his ideas and followed them with courage and judgment. This pattern could be seen in all of his business activities.

Early in life Goldman learned from his father the words of Disraeli: "The secret of success is constancy to purpose." Today, more than a hundred years since those words were penned, they still anchor Goldman. Ever since he started his business career he has kept on his desk a plaque that states: "I am a great believer in luck. The harder I work the more luck I seem to have."

But, if "luck" is the word, that luck has not all been good. The decade of the Roaring Twenties was a combination of boom and bust. The returning veterans of World War I donned civilian clothes at the beginning of a fabulous era that would prove unique in the American experience. Twenty-year-old Sylvan Goldman had little time to ponder this uniqueness, however. He needed employment immediately. His brother, Alfred, was ready with a suggestion. Alfred had enlisted in the army shortly after the younger Goldman and had been assigned to a training camp in Texas. But Alfred's military career progressed no further; army doctors discovered that he was suffering from mastoiditis, which affected his hearing in one ear. Learning of an opportunity in the wholesale grocery and produce business in San Antonio, he chose to stay in Texas after he was discharged. When the war ended and Sylvan returned, Alfred approached him with the idea of forming a partnership to establish a wholesale produce business in the Lone Star State. The two brothers turned to their uncle, Henry Dreyfus, for his opinion and possible financial backing. Dreyfus was readily convinced by their arguments. His nephews, although young men, could draw on a more than adequate background of experience in wholesale produce. They would have the additional advantage of what seemed to be an excellent location for their first business venture. Borrowing a page from the successful Dreyfus brothers' handbook, Alfred chose a developing oil-boom region approximately one hundred miles west of Fort Worth as the site for this enterprise. The prospect of profit appeared likely to Dreyfus, because there was no local wholesale produce company in that region to offer competition. He agreed to lend his nephews $5,000 to augment the savings that Alfred had accumulated.

Initially the Goldmans' plan proved sound. The rural communities in Cisco and Stephens counties were experiencing an intoxicating oil boom in the last half of 1919, when the brothers arrived in Texas. From a bankrupt poultry and egg dealer in Cisco they leased a building, equipped with refrigeration, to serve as a warehouse. With a cooler they could store fruits and vegetables shipped by rail from the Dallas–Fort Worth area. The Goldmans started by purchasing mixed shipments of produce from the large wholesale houses in the cities, since at first they did not have sufficient capital to buy in larger quantities directly from agricultural production centers. They sold to various customers in Cisco, including a hotel owned and managed by Conrad Hilton. It was the future hotel tycoon's first endeavor in the field he later came to dominate.

Sylvan Goldman's brother, Alfred (left), and a Goldman employee in front of the Goldman Brothers Wholesale Fruits and Produce in Breckenridge, Texas, in 1922. (Goldman Collection)

The Goldman brothers wanted to expand their business into surrounding villages, but their efforts were hampered by exceptionally poor dirt roads. Transportation was uncertain and, during rainy weather, virtually impossible. Luckily, a paved road connecting Cisco and Eastland was completed in 1920. The new road provided the young entrepreneurs with better access to their market: tiny grocery stores that had sprung up to meet the needs of the increased population resulting from oil strikes. As the only local

27

wholesalers available to these isolated stores, the Goldmans soon justified their faith in the project. It was not long until they began buying produce in carload lots directly from suppliers, just as larger wholesalers did. By January, 1921, Sylvan was handling the original territory, while Alfred had moved forty miles north to manage a branch at Breckenridge, where the biggest wells were being drilled. At that time, however, Breckenridge had to rely on trucks to deliver merchandise.

The nature of their undertaking left the brothers little time for relaxation and the enjoyment of profits. Most of their profits were put back into the business for expansion, including the purchase and maintenance of the large trucks needed for freighting. Because most of the business was transacted with small boom-town grocery stores, credit, at least on a weekly basis, had to be extended to many of them. Their proprietors demanded this service partly from necessity and partly out of the knowledge that difficult transport conditions allowed the wholesalers no alternative but to leave the perishable produce at the stores. As long as the oil wells kept pumping and new rigs kept going up, the roughnecks and roustabouts would remain and would need to buy groceries—and the Goldmans could collect on the previous order and take orders for the next delivery. Unfortunately, the smoothly running organization was dealt a staggering setback and eventually had to be dissolved when a faltering economy resulted in cutbacks in oil production.[1]

The United States had emerged from World War I as one of the strongest economic powers in the world. Although during the first half of 1919 national income and the output of goods dropped slightly from the peak of the war years, the nation's economy then surged ahead in a new business boom that lasted for some months. A high level of exports, made possible by American loans abroad and continued heavy spending by the federal government, accounted for this prosperity. By the middle of 1920, however, the business community began to slow, and within a few months the country was in the grip of a severe depression. The economic setback, resulting from inflation, unwise speculation, a decline in government spending, a steep drop in exports, and ruinous losses in farm income, brought thousands of business failures and left more than four million unemployed.[2]

The economy rebounded in 1922 and then continued on an almost uninterrupted high plane until 1929. But this improvement provided little comfort to the Goldmans, who were among the business casualties of 1921. Oil-field workers were laid off because of an oversupply of oil reserves and a consequent shutdown of drilling operations, and the booming towns of Cisco, Breckenridge, Ranger, Eastland, and smaller villages that the Goldmans served lost population almost as rapidly as they had grown. With shrinking numbers of customers the oil-town grocers closed their doors. All too frequently they hired a truck or two, loaded the store merchandise and whatever movable fixtures they could, and departed for more favorable locations, leaving behind nothing but unpaid bills and disappointed creditors, including the Goldmans. By the time the Goldmans had liquidated their holdings, paid off their bank loans, and left Texas, they had left no more than a small part of their own and their uncle's investment. They could count their profit only as the bitter taste of a melancholy experience.[3]

Unwilling to return to Oklahoma, the brothers looked elsewhere for a growing area that offered opportunity. Along with thousands of others, they turned west to California. That state's population growth outstripped all other states during the 1920's, and it, along with its East Coast rival, Florida, epitomized the real estate boom of that decade. In Los Angeles, Alfred easily found a position with a wholesale produce house, while Sylvan worked in a similar establishment that also handled groceries. Both jobs involved calling on retail merchants, a circumstance that inspired the brothers to think of opening their own grocery store some day. Neither possessed any experience in the retail field, but they believed their chances might be good if they could save enough money.

This optimism was soundly based. Grocery stores in California differed from those in most other parts of the country. Generally the grocery encompassed three separate businesses operating under a single roof. Fresh fruits and vegetables were handled by one department, usually as an independent concession. The Goldmans felt that they would be comfortable managing such an operation with their considerable background in the wholesale produce business; they were constrained, however, by the knowledge that Japanese-Americans held a near monopoly in that speciality. Meat markets had been joined under the same roof with other footstuffs, but they were owned and operated as separate entities, although some were chain operations. The third business in these early-day food markets was groceries—that is, any items not sold in the meat and produce departments. This method of operation was so common that many shopping-center developers soon began providing the permanent fixtures for grocery stores, eliminating the problem of dividing equipment among three concessions whose ownerships might change frequently.[4]

The Goldmans were planning their entry into the Los Angeles grocery business, as soon as they could save enough money, when they received an unexpected telephone call from Oklahoma. Their Uncle Henry Dreyfus was coming to California for an important conference with his nephews. On his arrival he advanced a proposition on behalf of the Dreyfus brothers' wholesale concern. The five brothers were prospering both in Tulsa and in their Sapulpa branch, which covered most of the territory within a one-hundred-mile area that included the new oil-field territory. For a number of years they had been working closely with a local grocer, who had developed a chain of stores in that territory, but the Dreyfus brothers had no financial interest in them. Nevertheless, rival wholesalers had spread rumors to other retail store owners that the Dreyfus brothers actually owned part of the chain. As a consequence, the wholesalers argued, if the retailers continued to order produce and groceries from the Dreyfus firm, they would really be buying from their competitor. On top of the drop in business that resulted from this tactic, the Dreyfus brothers were faced with a further problem when the grocer announced that he was building his own warehouse and would purchase his supplies directly from producers.

Caught in a dilemma not of their making, Dreyfus explained, his brothers had agreed that he should go to the West Coast with a proposition for the two nephews. With mounting enthusiasm the Goldmans listened to his proposal that they open and manage a grocery chain, backed by the Dreyfus brothers, in Tulsa. They would receive a 25 percent stock interest in the chain plus regular salaries. Dreyfus proposed financing them for a year while they made a study of the Los Angeles retail grocery scene to prepare them for opening and managing the stores.

With their Uncle Henry, the brothers spent several days in Los Angeles visiting the owners of three leading locally owned food-store chains. At first the owners were skeptical

Henry Dreyfus, the Goldman brothers' maternal uncle and financial partner. (Goldman Collection)

about outsiders working in various branches of their stores and going around with their supervisors to learn their accounting system. Henry Dreyfus told the owners that the two brothers would work without salary and that he would pay any expenses incurred in teaching them. However, the chain owners feared that Dreyfus and his nephews might try to use the knowledge they acquired to open a competing grocery business in California. Dreyfus was required to give proof of the kind of business he was in and where he operated. He also had to convince the chain operators that the reputation of the Dreyfus brothers was solid. Once the owners were certain the Goldmans had no intention of remaining in Los Angeles as competitors, they agreed to allow the two brothers to learn the business from the inside.

After putting their uncle on an eastbound train, the Goldmans started their year of study. Their curriculum embraced a wide range of subjects. Spending four months with each chain, they worked in all departments incorporated in each store. They served as clerks, filling customers' orders from behind the counters and collecting for the groceries, produce, and meat purchases, which were paid for at the separate departments in each store. A few grocers in the Los Angeles area had begun the self-service operation, and the Goldmans observed the different procedures involved with that innovation. They met with supervisors, meat managers, produce men, and executives. They even helped with the myriad details of opening a new store. After about a year the brothers felt confident that they were knowledgeable in every aspect of the retail grocery business except one: the use of their skills and knowledge in their own endeavor. They returned to Oklahoma eager to find out what they could do.[5]

On April 3, 1926, the Goldmans opened their first grocery

store, the Sun Grocery, at 1403 East Fifteenth Street in Tulsa. A year later there were twenty-one Sun Grocery Company stores to celebrate the first anniversary. The orange-and-black storefronts of the chain had become well known everywhere in Tulsa, for the Goldmans had spread their rising-sun symbol to all parts of town. When a new store opened, the headline of their advertisement read, "A new Sun rises today." This extraordinarily rapid expansion had been spurred by the realization that the Dreyfus brothers would lose customers in direct ratio to the frequency with which any other chain opened competitive stores.

Sylvan Goldman headed the company as president, while Alfred served as vice-president. The amazing rate of expansion of Sun grocery stores brought the two brothers to almost immediate local prominence. They were applying the business techniques they had learned in California with the zeal of devoted converts. Virtually every phase of their organization reflected a firm grasp of current retail management principles plus a willingness to experiment with promising new concepts. The abilities of each brother neatly complemented those of the other. Sylvan was the more aggressive and outgoing of the two, but he was balanced by Alfred, who was quiet, reserved, and especially gifted in planning and analysis of the inner workings of their business. Both possessed a keen sense of humor and charm that were undiminished by a highly disciplined work ethic.

As vice-president of the company Alfred assumed the responsibilities of general office management of the stores. He was also in charge of the firm's purchasing agents, who bought the many items stocked in each unit. Sylvan handled general store supervision and operation plus the overseeing of all the department supervisors. The two brothers

The first Sun Store in Tulsa, Oklahoma, was a service store where customers were waited on. This picture was taken about 1926. (Goldman Collection)

always agreed on new store locations before any steps toward acquisition were made. They invariably picked high-traffic areas, trying to avoid less frequented side streets. They built their stores of brick, both for its resistance to fire and its neat appearance. Two-thirds of the buildings in the chain were new; others were opened in existing structures.[6]

In addition to their normal executive functions, the brothers prepared all the newspaper advertising themselves, and they supervised the handling of their merchandising concepts in actual store operations. Much of the success of the Sun Grocery chain and of the Goldmans' later business ventures can be attributed to their clear understanding of customers' desires. The food industry has always been particularly susceptible to advertising gambits. That others in the field appreciated this fact cannot be doubted, yet few were able to capitalize on this knowledge as effectively as the Goldmans did.

Providing food for the country's mealtimes placed the nation's food merchants in the first position among American industries in terms of product value during the 1920's. In dollar volume of production the food processors, wholesalers, and retailers comprised a $12.7 billion industry in 1919, $3.5 billion more than second-ranked textiles and textile products. Ten years later the food industry's dollar volume was still in first position. The feeding of Americans was the ranking business during the decade and was also one in which there was tremendous competition for the purchasing dollar.[7]

"The wonderful thing about food from our point of view," a food industry executive of a later era commented, "is that everybody uses it—and uses it only once."[8] Food vendors have had a substantial advantage in selling their product, an advantage most other retailers have not enjoyed. Purchased items either were consumed or perished, and merchants could depend on a rhythm in the buying patterns of most customers, who replenished their food stocks at calculable intervals. Until the post–World War I period there were remarkably few changes in food distribution. During the following decade, however, four important

Employees in one of the first self-service Sun Stores in Tulsa, Oklahoma, 1927. The first four stores in the chain were service stores, but the fifth store and all others thereafter were self-service stores. (Goldman Collection)

developments took place that revolutionized the retailing aspect of the food industry: the phenomenal growth of chain-store operations; an increasing acceptance of self-service in groceries, later expanding into food items; an enlargement of individual retail outlet sizes; and a widening of merchandizing to include nonfood items.[9]

That the youthful president and vice-president of Sun Grocery Company were knowledgeable about the latest trends in their field was obvious. They did not yet include nonfood items in their chain stores—an innovation introduced but not widely accepted in the 1920's—otherwise their business practices were in the forefront of the movement to modernize the retail grocery business.They did not simply follow where others had blazed a trail but consistently adhered to the advice they would later offer the next generation: "The two main foundations a young man should have are lots of horse sense and a liking for the job he is doing." [10]

The nature and success of the Goldman chain in Tulsa reflected how well those foundations served the brothers. The trend, beginning slowly in the period 1920 to 1925, was toward larger grocery stores that handled fresh meats and produce in addition to a line of groceries. Conforming to this pattern, the Sun Grocery stores averaged close to five thousand square feet of selling space, which was larger than most Oklahoma grocery stores of that era. Although combining the produce, meat, and grocery concessions under a single roof did not constitute a revolutionary idea, the brothers did change the retail operation to self-service, and their customers paid for purchases at a check stand.

Yet these changes and innovations alone did not account for the Goldmans' success. It was the Goldmans' merchandising talents that brought unusual success to the Sun chain. Advertisers had not yet begun studying the impact and influence of their efforts on people's buying habits. During the decade of the 1920's, however, advertising was a growing means of merchandising goods. The Goldmans believed especially in the potency of newspaper advertising, their prime means of reaching potential customers during that decade. But they were also knowledgeable about human nature in other ways. For example, they chose their company name carefully: Sun, a single-syllable word easily remembered, one with pleasant connotations, and one allowing the use of the striking orange-and-black storefront motif. Their newspaper advertisements and handbills depicted a just-rising sun with an inscription informing the reader that Sun Grocery Company was the "Most Economical Under the Sun."[11] Economy was the key word in most of the Goldmans' advertising copy. They employed that theme in many imaginative ways to show the public that the Sun Company's policies were aimed at providing the lowest possible prices for food items. Advertising columns stressed that volume buying made it possible for Sun to sell more cheaply to the consumer. This message was relayed subtly and obliquely in a passage from the Goldmans' interview on their first anniversary: "Quality is the first thing we consider in our purchases. Our enormous buying power takes care of the prices."[12]

The emphasis on economy was designed to educate the public to accept an innovation that the Sun Company borrowed from other chain operations—self-service. The first step taken by the Sun Grocery chain toward this method, which was to cause a basic change in many retail businesses, was a contest. The company offered $150 in prizes for winning slogans stating, in twenty-five words or less, why the Sun Stores' policy of "no delivery" meant money saved to grocery buyers.[13] Many shoppers had the habit of telephoning their food needs to grocers and leaving to store personnel the responsibility for gathering the items and carting them to the customers' homes. Other customers were accustomed to buying on credit, a practice also dis-

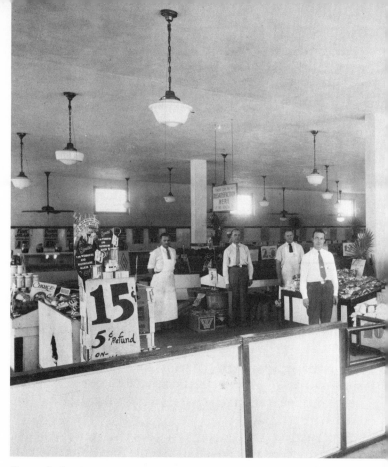

One of the largest self-service Sun Grocery stores in Tulsa. (Goldman Collection)

continued at Sun stores. The Goldmans' contest was aimed at relieving their chain from these time-consuming and expensive tasks while providing excellent publicity emphasizing the steps taken by the Sun Company to save its customers money.

During the chain's second year of operation, the

Goldmans' new stores were all self-service operations. There was some customer resistance to this concept; some people felt that gathering their own groceries was demeaning. Most customers, however, quickly became accustomed to the new method of shopping. Also during this period the Sun Company's expansion program outstripped its first year's accomplishments. Looking beyond the boundaries of metropolitan Tulsa, the Goldmans decided to widen the territory served by the orange-and-black stores to a number of smaller communities. By the spring of 1928, Sun stores had opened in towns extending southward from Tulsa to Henryetta, fifty-five miles away, and including Kiefer, Mounds, and Beggs. A second line reached as far southwest as Chandler and featured stores in Sapulpa, Bristow, Stroud, and other towns. The chain boasted fifty stores after a little more than two years in business.[14]

The Goldman brothers had justified their uncles' faith in their ability to apply the lessons they learned from their year's work in California. They had consistently used the latest techniques in building the Sun chain. Yet one reason for their phenomenal success had little or no connection with modernizing ideas. It came from the enlightened personnel policy laid out by the company's chief executives: efficiency in the work force became a hallmark of all the Goldmans' later enterprises. By the time it reached its maximum growth level, the chain employed large numbers of persons.

The Goldmans' progressive theories were also manifested in the Sun Company's policy regarding promotion. Virtually all the firm's executive and managerial positions were filled by men who had been recruited from among the company's employees. A. K. Weiss, a cousin of the Goldmans, was secretary-treasurer; Charles Nachtmann was head of the meat operation; Scott A. Millis was grocery supervisor, and M. P. Green was office manager. Nachtmann was the only one of the four who had had substantial experience in the grocery business, and he was also the only man over forty. In his years as an independent store operator and later as meat-market manager for other stores, he had gained a reputation for dealing in high-quality meat. That was what the Goldmans wanted; in fact, they considered Nachtmann's experience absolutely necessary, because the meat operation was the area in which the two top Sun executives had the least knowledge. Nachtmann was given complete control over that department.

Scott Millis began as a grocery clerk in the first Sun store about a month after it opened. When the sixth unit of the chain opened, he was named assistant store manager and later manager. In time he became the Goldmans' first store supervisor. In this job Millis served as middleman between the main office and the individual store managers.

Obviously the Goldmans kept a close watch on their employees, looking for those who had the potential to assume greater responsibilities. Perhaps the major strength of this practice was the young president's consistent open-mindedness: he refused to categorize any employee as locked in a lifetime position if he had untapped ability that could be drawn out. Goldman's flexibility was unusual for his time. To fill Millis' former position as manager of the sixth store, he broke one of his original company rules by selecting the person he believed best qualified, a woman. Alice Millis, the wife of Goldman's newest executive, had worked for some time as a grocery clerk. She proved an able and businesslike manager during a period when "liberated women" (an unheard-of term) were thought of as flappers, daringly experimenting with short skirts, cigarettes, bootleg gin, and pseudo-Freudian free love.[15]

By December, 1928, the highly successful young leaders of the Sun Grocery Company must have been feeling a certain satisfaction with life. In a short time they had fashioned a chain of fifty-five stores, most of which were profiting in an era of pork chops at twenty-nine cents a pound, potatoes at ten cents a pound, and bacon at forty-two cents a pound.[16] The Goldmans were thus decidedly unprepared for the appearance one morning of a man who announced his intention of buying them out—stores, warehouse, name, everything. At first refusing to reveal his financial backing, the man finally convinced the two brothers that his proposal was serious. The Goldmans consulted their uncles, who expressed an interest in selling if the transaction was enlarged to include the wholesale business. When confronted with this counterproposal, the buyer listened equably—and almost immediately accepted the new condition. After some brief bargaining sessions with the Dreyfus brothers and the Goldmans, the agreement was made in January, 1929.

Under the terms of the purchase contract the buyer, now revealed as Skaggs-Safeway Stores, agreed to a specified price for the Sun Grocery Company. In a companion sale the Dreyfus brothers' wholesale firm was acquired by a subsidiary of Safeway, the Western States Grocery Company. Although it was one of the nation's largest grocery chains, Safeway had not previously entered the retail market in Oklahoma. The company representative in these negotiations insisted that the Goldmans remain with the Tulsa organization until the takeover was accomplished. For the next six months the former president and vice-president of Sun Grocery acted as Safeway's Oklahoma manager and assistant manager, respectively. The name of the stores was changed to Safeway, but the orange-and-black fronts were retained.

If the Goldmans had any regrets about the sale, their share of the purchase price and the conditions under which it was paid undoubtedly lessened them. The Dreyfus brothers and the Goldmans had agreed to an arrangement through which they would receive shares of Safeway common stock in exchange for their interests. The New York Stock Exchange listed Safeway Stores at $140 a share when the sale was negotiated in January. Delivery of the stock issue, however, was not to be executed until an inventory and an audit were completed by the second week of March, 1929. If Safeway stock declined in the interval, more shares would be added to the stock issues to make up for any loss incurred since January. In the event that the stock exchange quoted a higher price for the Safeway listing in March, the sellers would realize an advantage from the increased value of their shares. Thanks to the wildly bullish market of early 1929, the Dreyfus-Goldman group received its Safeway stock at a price that provided a profit of $20 a share, and by September of that year it had risen to about $195 a share.[17]

The Goldmans suddenly felt wealthy with this 25 percent interest in the Sun Company. In that spring of 1929 they had been transformed from hardworking grocery executives to monied stockholders. Not surprisingly, they immediately received plenty of advice on the correct care and handling of their budding fortune. The stockbrokers who answered the young men's daily inquiries about the health of their Safeway shares offered the benefit of their experience. They cautioned the brothers not to leave all their financial eggs in one basket; diversification of their investments would prove to be a sage course. This counsel seemed to be exceptionally logical and was easily facilitated by the sale of part of their Safeway holdings and reinvestment in several blue-chip stocks.

Two or three weeks spent in observing the continual upward trend of the stock exchange dispelled any doubts the brothers entertained concerning another suggestion their broker made. If the Goldmans wanted to take full advantage of the current bull market, he urged, they should trade on margin. Under this arrangement the stock buyer was relieved of the burden of putting up the full purchase price for his orders for securities. Instead, the broker accepted a cash percentage of the actual price of stocks from the buyer, who hoped to pay the balance of the purchase at a future date with the earnings of the stock's rise on the exchange. The Goldmans could pay 10 percent down on each one-hundred-dollar stock order and let the rising market and resulting dividends take care of the remaining purchase price some months later. Naturally, if the market price of their shares fell during the scheduled time period, they would have to pay the balance from their own pockets.[18] Fortunately, even in the face of the overwhelming temptation presented by the market in 1929, the brothers did not want to take such a gamble. Their broker argued that stocks would not drop 50 percent and so the brothers would not be taking a great gamble; they could have 50 percent more stock without paying any more money. The Goldmans finally decided to keep about 25 percent of their Safeway stock aside and trade with the balance of their stock on margin, using the 50 percent margin limit on the purchase of other securities.

With this financial compromise completed, the two decided that they had earned a respite from business. Their father and mother had remained in Tulsa only a short time when they moved from Ardmore in 1913. They had then moved to Bartlesville and opened a dry-goods store, which they operated until the mid-1920's, when they sold it and returned to Tulsa. They had purchased profitable investment properties, and Goldman senior retired. Thus, when Alfred and Sylvan decided that a trip to the Pacific Coast would be relaxing and might offer an interesting opportunity for investment, the jaunt became a family affair with their parents and Uncle Henry Dreyfus accompanying them.

After a leisurely trip across the western United States, the two-car caravan arrived in Los Angeles, where the group enjoyed visits with relatives and friends and a drive south on a sightseeing tour as far as Tijuana. Back in Los Angeles at a dinner party, the brothers and their uncle were introduced to the owners of a small, cut-rate retail drug chain. It seemed that the drug chain was prospering, but there was one flaw in its operation that concerned the owners. The chain was not sufficiently large to have the sales volume needed to buy directly from drug manufacturers in wholesale quantities; thus it was forced to deal with profit-reducing middlemen.

Familiar with the Oklahomans' huge success, and learning of their search for a new field of investment, the drugstore merchants eagerly submitted the suggestion that the two groups should join forces. If the Oklahoma grocers would use some of their capital to start a cut-rate drug chain outside California, then all of them could pool their purchasing resources and supply their stores at wholesale prices. The venture sounded plausible to Dreyfus, and his nephews agreed. The drugstore business, they believed, would be simple in comparison to the intricacies of the retail food line. Once stocked, a drugstore virtually ran itself without the worries of spoilage, produce procurement, and meat marketing that demanded so much time in the grocery business.

With the idea of expanding their potential market, Sylvan, Alfred, and their uncle took their new friends' advice and headed north to Oregon and Washington to search for possible store sites if the area looked promising. The Goldmans' mother and father remained in Los Angeles to vacation with relatives. If successful, the three travelers would begin operations by which they could use the pool-buying arrangement. None of the tourists had visited Oregon or Washington before, and they combined business with pleasure by observing the scenery as they scouted the region for possible sites for drugstores. At regular intervals the Goldmans bought newspapers, hurriedly turning to the financial pages to relish the stock quotations, which continued their gratifying upward spiral of the past several months.

Labor Day found the Oklahomans in Vancouver, enjoying that Canadian resort area. Then, beginning their return trip south, they stopped in Seattle to pursue their haphazard search for possible store sites. Near the city's public market, to which the seasoned produce men from Tulsa naturally gravitated, they spotted an excellent possibility. A large for-lease sign was in the empty show window of an equally barren store standing advantageously between two busy thoroughfares in the downtown area.

Inquiries led them to the lawyer handling the property for its absentee owner, who lived in the East. An hour's questioning convinced the Oklahomans that the store would serve admirably as the site for their first drugstore. Accordingly, they agreed on a ten-year lease. The attorney suggested that he dictate the lease while the four of them discussed it item by item, which would save the time of retyping the agreement several times. When this process was completed, the lawyer invited them to lunch while his secretary typed the final form. After lunch, they were to close the agreement by signing the document, for the lawyer explained that he was empowered by the property owner to complete any lease arrangement. The four men went to the attorney's club for lunch, and among the topics inevitably discussed during the meal was the weather. The Oklahomans made much of the beautiful, mild climate of Washington in August and September compared with the hot, dusty days at home at the end of summer. Their host acknowledged the pleasant state of the season and noted that it would continue to be good until November, when Seattle's "dry rain" would begin. Puzzled, his guests questioned the attorney about this apparently contradictory term. It was not a great mystery, the lawyer explained: "Dry rain" was the local residents' half-humorous description of the moisture-laden mist that dominated Seattle's atmosphere from late autumn to February each year.

The Goldmans and their uncle exchanged glances and then calmly informed the lawyer that they could not sign the lease. They explained that both Alfred Goldman and Henry Dreyfus had arthritis, a condition greatly aggravated by prolonged exposure to damp weather. Rather abruptly the Tulsans' plans for forging a chain of drugstores in league with their friends in Los Angeles were halted. The latter had already expressed their intention of extending their operations to San Francisco, while their would-be partners had agreed to position themselves north of that city. Explanations and good-bys completed, the two-car family caravan left Los Angeles early in September. Uncle Henry Dreyfus and the Goldman brothers were relieved at the peculiar manner in which they had escaped what could have been a very expensive investment in Seattle. On the way home they consoled themselves by reading reports of the still-rising stock market.

Within weeks of their return to Oklahoma the two would regard that institution less calmly.[19] On Thursday, October

24, 1929, the first of several financial jolts startled the nation. The stock exchange rallied that day from a frightening low, but the recovery was short-lived. Five days later the New York stock market experienced the most devastating twenty-four hours in its history: the awesome "Black Tuesday" crash. Succeeding days and weeks failed to bring a halt to the decline of the market and, eventually, of the national economy. Those who remained optimistic during the waning days of autumn discovered that the boom decade had ended; the era of boundless faith in the ultimate progress of the United States had disappeared by Christmas.

In Tulsa the Goldmans were among those who tried to weather the storm by hanging onto their investments. They finally sold their portfolio after the great crash, having borrowed money to meet margin demands. Between them the brothers retained about $25,000 of the more than $300,000 they had received in stock from the sale of the Sun stores.[20] In the decade of the 1920's they had built two successful businesses and suffered two dismal busts. They had proved that they could prosper in good times. Late in 1929 they were faced with earning a living in bad times.

3. Making a Living During the Depression

Sylvan Goldman and his brother Alfred had amassed considerable wealth at relatively young ages through hard work and applied knowledge. The stock-market crash, which reduced their affluence to a fraction of its original level, had dealt the same blow to older, more experienced men. Not especially comforted by the thought that they had salvaged something from the disaster and that their stocks had continued to drop after they had been sold, the two young Oklahomans contemplated ways and means of rebuilding their fortune. The incredible recovery they achieved in the midst of America's worst depression can be attributed to their determination to capitalize through ever-harder work on the opportunities available and on their never-diminishing efforts to force bad luck to reverse itself.

No one seriously doubted that the United States was actually in a depression by the winter of 1929–30. So many businesses had closed that a grim joke suggested that the only people making money were those who owned tall buildings: they rented rooms to those who were jumping out of windows after ruin in the collapsing stock market.[1] As the Depression wore on, contradicting the opinions of many that it would be of short duration, such stories became less humorous. For the overwhelming majority of citizens the American dream dissolved abruptly into nightmare. The security and happiness they expected as a reward for thrift and hard work disappeared; the seemingly endless vista of continuous prosperity faded into the reality of lost savings, unemployment, foreclosed mortgages, and evictions. Poverty, a condition thought to exist in only isolated pockets of the nation, became evident everywhere in alarming proportions. As the depression showed no signs of lessening, many people surrendered to a numbing despair. Only gradually would the nation regain the confidence it lost in the early years of the depression.

Sylvan and Alfred Goldman reacted to the adversity of the times by moving to another area of the state. Hundreds of thousands of Americans eventually did the same, although few converted their geographical relocation so profitably. Actually the brothers had little choice in leaving Tulsa if they wanted to reenter the grocery business. Part of the purchase agreement they had signed with Safeway in 1929 stipulated that they could not establish a grocery store in any community where the Sun chain had operated. The selling contract had specified originally that the restriction would last for ten years, but Safeway's legal staff had advised the company that a five-year maximum existed on such contracts. Two possibilities presented themselves to the Goldman brothers in 1929. Oil fields around Shawnee, Bowlegs, Shamrock, and Weleetka in east-central Oklahoma had brought a boom economy which could be profitable to a grocery chain. The Goldmans, however, were unable to secure the bankrupt chain offered for sale in those towns. They were left with their next geographical choice, Oklahoma City.[2]

In this third major business venture the brothers had additional responsibilities. Before the stock-market crash they had attended a cousin's engagement party in Tulsa. The cousin had arranged for the Goldmans to escort two of

Margaret ("Babe") Katz Goldman, Sylvan's wife. (Goldman Collection)

her friends from out of town, Margaret and Helen Katz, of Stillwater, Oklahoma. The girls' father, Jake Katz, owned and operated a department store which he had opened in that town in the 1890's. After a pleasant evening the brothers asked the Katz sisters to join them at their cousin's wedding; their invitation was accepted. The two couples, Alfred and Helen, Sylvan and Margaret, then dated occasionally until the Goldmans sold the Sun stores and left for California. In 1929, despite the financial problems preoccupying the brothers' thoughts, Alfred found time to renew his acquaintance with Helen Katz. The two were married before the end of the year—in time for the bride to make the move with him to Oklahoma City.

Margaret Katz came from Stillwater often to visit her sister—which gave Sylvan a chance to see her. These trips grew more and more frequent, and Sylvan remembers on one date, at a propitious moment, she turned to him and said, "Well, aren't you going to kiss me? I'm going to marry you." Sylvan says he was not really surprised, for he had the same thought, but he told her he was in such a financial straits from the rebuilding effort that he could not buy her face powder. Her immediate response was, "I won't use it." They were married on his brother Alfred's birthday, June 7, 1931. Two sons were born to them, Monte in 1936 and Alfred in 1938. Margaret, the youngest child in her family, had always been called "Baby" at home. Ever since her marriage she has been "Babe" to an ever-widening circle of friends around the world.[3]

When the Goldman brothers moved to Oklahoma City, it was the largest city in the state and thus a good potential market. But, the latecoming Tulsans felt some trepidation about their move. The pall of depression which hung over the nation also was casting a dark shadow over Oklahoma

Morris Dreyfus, the Goldman brothers' maternal uncle and business partner in Oklahoma City. (Goldman Collection)

City. Competition was not lacking either, with the presence of Piggly Wiggly, Kroger, and Safeway food chains—three of the country's largest—in addition to many independent stores and smaller chains. Obviously the Goldman brothers would need every ounce of energy and expertise to succeed in this far-from-promising market.

After marshaling their resources, the two then asked their uncles, Morris and Henry Dreyfus, to join them in the venture in Oklahoma City. Morris assumed an active role in the new business, while Henry provided some financial support but stayed in Tulsa. The family spent most of its capital to buy five small grocery stores from a bankrupt chain. Four of the buildings, which had twenty-five-foot fronts, were in the suburbs, while the fifth was downtown, on the corner of Robinson and Reno streets.

The Goldmans gave the suburban stores the name Sunshine stores after a customer contest to choose a suitable name to go with the fresh coats of bright-yellow paint that adorned the storefronts.[4] The downtown store was named Standard and had a separate identity from the suburban locations.[5] All the buildings were small compared with later designs; the Standard store had a mere twenty-five feet by fifty feet of sales area, although it did have a basement for storage. None of the stores had parking facilities, a condition which influenced the Goldmans to offer free delivery service from the suburban locations. The brothers reasoned that boys on bicycles could deliver groceries and build business during the hard times when potential customers were reluctant to use their automobiles—if they still owned them. As soon as possible the brothers phased out this obsolete service, which contradicted their concept of retail operations. Initially, however, it was a good business practice for the small Sunshine stores.

Necessity also dictated other policies for each store in the chain. All sales were for cash. The money pinch presented the Goldmans with another problem that required a special stratagem. If the new chain was to compete with established businesses, competitive prices would be necessary. They had to persuade the wholesale grocers of Oklahoma City to give them discount prices on their orders; this would allow the Goldmans to sell as cheaply as chain stores and to attain a competitive position. Unfortunately, the five stores did not have enough buying volume to warrant such an arrangement. The single bit of leverage the Goldmans had was their family's reputation. Oklahoma City wholesalers were keenly aware of the new chain owners' record in Tulsa as wholesale and retail operators. With this fact in mind, the Goldmans asked Oklahoma City wholesalers about the possibility of continuous buying at a discount. When they encountered reluctance, they hinted that their uncles might establish their own wholesale house in the city. The plan worked perfectly. The wholesalers had no way of knowing that neither the Dreyfus brothers nor the Goldmans commanded sufficient funds to back this bluff. The wholesalers who provided this advantage lost nothing in the process, for they had only to alter their delivery routes slightly to include the new customers.

Despite the success of this arrangement, the Goldmans still faced an additional obstacle—paying their weekly bills. The situation called for an unusual commercial move. Noting that wholesalers normally allowed ten days for payment for delivered items, the Goldmans began switching suppliers, ordering groceries from one firm one week and another the following week. This enabled them to meet their credit deadlines by using their receipts from the previous week's purchases from a different wholesaler during each ten-day grace period, but paying all bills as they came due.[6]

Obtaining goods at an advantageous price proved complicated, and the effort would be totally wasted unless customers could be persuaded to buy the groceries. Before people could buy the stores' products, they had to be made aware that they were available. With the Goldmans' past achievements in advertising, there should have been no great difficulty in this area. However, once again funds— or, more accurately, an insufficiency of funds—caused the Goldmans and their uncles to seek a substitute for the preferred but expensive newspaper medium. They substituted floods of handbills touting the stores' superior quality, low prices, and free delivery. To supplement the handbills, the Goldmans instructed company personnel to use the stores themselves as billboards, painting show windows with the news that bananas could be purchased at three cents a pound, oranges at fifteen cents a dozen, lettuce at five cents a head, and so on.[7]

The bitter winds of the Great Depression were blowing with ever-increasing intensity in Oklahoma City in early 1931. On January 20 hundreds of unemployed men gathered at the corner of Reno and Robinson, site of the Goldmans' Standard store, to begin a march on City Hall, then situated two blocks north at Grand and Robinson. Before the embittered, cold, hungry men could be assembled, the sight of groceries turned them into a leaderless mob, and they crashed through the windows to pillage the small store. In only minutes they left it in a shambles, another costly blow for the Goldmans to overcome.

The remarkable aspect of this developing food chain, other than its continued existence in the middle of the Depression, was its constant growth and expansion.

The first Standard Food Store in Oklahoma City, at 130 West Reno Avenue, in 1930. (Goldman Collection.

Goldman never paused to reflect on the possible dire consequences of reinvesting profits during a period of general economic retrenchment. Possessing a determined self-confidence, he formulated his financial philosophy. On the subject of going into debt for business purposes, Sylvan recommended borrowing all the funds available "if you

The store at 130 West Reno Avenue after it was pillaged in 1931 by a bitter mob of unemployed men. (Goldman Collection)

know what to do with the money and how to invest it properly and profitably." In the same optimistic vein he decried the fear of powerful competitors such as those he and his brother faced in the 1930's. He suggested, "It isn't the size of a company that counts, but the advantages of being flexible, using good judgment and being able to grab opportunities while larger operations must debate or wait on company routine and red tape for decisions."[8]

There was nothing about the Goldmans' beginnings that could be termed indecisive or cautious. As the Sunshine leases expired, the stores were either renovated and enlarged or moved to better locations. At the same time they were renamed Standard Food Markets and became self-service stores. The free-delivery feature was dropped. Emphasis was placed on reducing costs to maintain low prices, which meant effecting radical changes in traditional concepts of grocery management. The brothers' experiments in Tulsa during the 1920's had been directed toward conditioning shoppers to self-service. Ironically, the Depression, by fostering an acute awareness of all price variations, actually aided in the development of modern food markets.

Each remodeling, relocation, or enlargement of the five original stores brought innovations in retail food merchandising. In August, 1933, a store in the Farmer's Public Market was for lease. It came with all store equipment and a bakery, which the Goldmans enlarged to produce a large variety of bakery products for their Standard stores. By baking bread in large quantities, they were able to sell it for five cents a loaf. The price attracted customers to the stores, and although the stores made no direct profit on the bread, volume trade justified the tactic.

When they took over the Public Market Store, their father came out of retirement and worked for them intermittently as cashier in the large meat department. In his final years it was a joy for him to visit with the many customers. Michael Goldman died on March 21, 1945.

In 1934, Standard built the first of its large markets. The floor space, 50 by 140 feet, was enhanced by a large parking

The Goldman brothers, Alfred (left) and Sylvan, 1934. (Goldman Collection)

lot. Built in a residential area of Oklahoma City, the store reflected a national trend to larger suburban outlets. Spacious parking facilities stimulated the customers' growing tendency to drive to market and carry home large supplies of groceries.[9]

While these improvements in facilities were important,

primarily they were adaptations of what other retailers were doing across the nation. The Goldmans, however, were among those who pioneered self-service produce departments. The preeminence of Standard stores in this aspect of food retailing was acknowledged in 1938, when a national trade magazine, *Super Market Merchandising*, asked Sylvan to contribute an article on the subject. In it he explained much of the Goldman philosophy about self-service stores, and he discussed the use of this concept in produce merchandising. According to the Goldmans, self-service departments were practical and profitable because they increased volume while reducing labor and operating costs. Customers could browse through the fruits and vegetables and choose whatever looked tempting. They did not have to rely on a clerk's judgment.

Sylvan's article anticipated the major objection of many grocery managers to self-service produce sections—the tomato squeezer. He labeled as groundless the fear that enormous losses would be incurred because of customers who manhandled fruits and vegetables. Sylvan suggested that to counteract this threat and to maintain a smooth-running department, store owners should stress proper training for the produce managers who graded, priced, and displayed fragile items. The article suggested that checkers and sackers prepare the produce in the early morning during slow business hours, thus offsetting inefficiency in labor use. Goldman asserted that eventually all stores would be forced by competition to adopt the new method.[10] He was correct.

In 1934 the Goldmans' program of expansion continued with the purchase of five self-service Humpty Dumpty stores that had been the Goldmans' major competitors, but had gone bankrupt. However, the properties had to be

One of the Goldmans' first large self-service stores in Oklahoma City. (Goldman Collection)

acquired through a receivership sale. The Goldmans and their uncles did not have the necessary capital to bid for them, so the Goldmans went to the different wholesale grocery suppliers in Oklahoma City, who they were sure were Humpty Dumpty's largest creditors, and told them that if the Goldmans did not buy these stores at auction, then Safeway, Kroger, or another chain like A&P would be the only ones able to purchase them. Then the wholesalers would not get any of the stores' business, for all these chains had their own warehouses and bought their merchandise direct, just as the wholesalers did. If the Goldmans could bid for these stores and buy them, they could not pay the wholesalers any cash, but would repay the loan from the profits derived from the stores. After considerable persuasion, the wholesalers agreed, and the Goldmans successfully bid on the stores at the auction.

The new stores retained their name and were operated as competitors to the other Goldman stores. In actuality they were centrally managed and directed by the Goldmans, although they were two separate corporations. Not until 1943, when a shortage of newsprint prompted the decision to merge advertising space for Standard and Humpty Dumpty stores, did people learn that the two groups of stores were associated. Much of the chain's expansion after World War II came under the Humpty Dumpty name.[11]

To the Goldmans the name Humpty Dumpty seemed more suitable for the type of stores they were developing in the 1930's and 1940's. To some it appeared odd that, despite the Goldmans' obviously growing chain, they were operating fewer stores in Oklahoma City after ten years than they were in Tulsa after three years during the 1920's. The answer lay not in the Depression but in the size of the stores and a shortage of funds. In 1938, Sylvan erected his first out-of-town unit at Shawnee. This store, with its large parking lot, could only be described as a "supermarket." In their trend to larger stores the Goldmans were pioneering in what in the next decade would become a revolution in the retail food industry, although others would receive most of the credit for this change.

California and Texas furnished social and economic climates friendly to the development of supermarkets. In the 1920's Ralph's Grocery Company, Carty Brothers, and Alpha Beta Food Markets built retail stores in California that were entitled to use the appellation "super," although they did not. In Texas, ABC Stores operated supermarket prototypes by the early 1920's. Later that decade, store and chain owners in both areas began using the term "supermarket" to describe their operations. However, the term did not become a corporate or trade name until 1933. Despite their early and attractive appearance, these southwestern stores failed to attract attention by their presence, as did the Depression-decade supermarkets developed in New York and New Jersey. Michael Cullen, formerly an executive with the Kroger organization, opened the first of what one author called the "cheapy" supermarket. Cullen rented vacant manufacturing buildings on the outskirts of cities where ample parking was available. These stores were gigantic enterprises featuring low prices, crude interiors, and flamboyant advertising. Cullen's fantastic success with his first store in Flushing, New York, resulted in a chain of King Kullen Markets that, before his death in 1936, sold every type of merchandise.[12]

In the neighboring state of New Jersey came the beginning and growth of a similar operation that received nationwide notice and powerfully influenced the growth of the supermarket industry. Robert M. Otis and Roy O. Dawson leased a vacant automobile plant in Elizabeth, New Jersey, in 1932. There they used fifty thousand square feet of space to sell groceries and other merchandise at low prices. Supermarkets were never mentioned in typical advertisements. Instead, the company name was exploited so that the chain stores always "crushed," "slashed," "banged," and "crashed" prices to amazingly low levels. Specially marked items were invariably "sensational," "colossal," "stupendous," or "the lowest" buys available. The chain itself claimed preeminence as "America's Greatest Thrift Center" or "World's Champion Price Fighter," where millions "shop and save" because the market had "no high-salaried executives," "no large overhead," "no fancy frills or fixtures," and "all your needs under one roof." At the end of one year's operation the New Jersey Big Bear organization had drawn five million customers to its original store. This figure, by itself, indicated the effectiveness of the advertising, which became so familiar through imitation. Actually these stores sold their groceries below cost. Their profits came from rent collected from separate concessions housed under the same roof, such as variety, drug, ready-to-war, restaurant, and dry goods. Ordinarily customers seeking grocery bargains were first exposed to other wares displayed in the front areas. Foodstuffs were strategically located in the rear.[13]

For the average citizen struggling with the Depression, it was enough that the supermarkets offered lower grocery prices. In Oklahoma City the Goldmans and their competitors were striving to gain their share of the public's food dollar. If Standard–Humpty Dumpty thrived, much of its success was because of the Goldmans' willingness to adapt others' merchandising advances and the brothers' ability to develop their own innovations.[14]

The steady but spectacular growth of the Goldman food chain belied much of the real difficulty Sylvan and his partners encountered in the Depression atmosphere of Oklahoma. One of their more perplexing problems had its origin in the banking crisis of 1933, coupled with subsequent attempts by the federal government to change the alarming effects of that crisis on the economy. The governor of Nevada had closed his state's banks in October, 1932, when it became apparent that they might collapse. During the next two months, bank failures in other western states contributed to a growing awareness that a new financial disaster similar to the stock market crash of 1929 might be imminent. This premonition became a harsh reality at the end of the following February and the beginning of March. Banks were failing across the nation, causing the governors of thirty-eight states to halt financial activities. Franklin D. Roosevelt, impatiently awaiting his inauguration on March 4, had already publicly expressed concern that the economic structure of the nation seemed unlikely to hold together until he could take office. Much of the nation shared his feelings, as news of continuing bank failures was interspersed with ominous reports of corporate failures and the commodity markets closing in New York, Chicago, and Kansas City.

Oklahoma Governor William H. Murray joined his counterparts in California, Louisiana, and Alabama as they closed their respective states' banks on the night of March 1. Four days later President Roosevelt declared a national bank "holiday," a fortunate euphemism which in itself did something to relieve people's tension. Nevertheless, no one knew when the country's financial system would reopen or under what circumstances. The few days it took Roosevelt and Congress to fashion a new banking law were uneasy ones for many people. Ingenious methods, designed to carry on normal activities without money, were devised. Some northern states accepted Canadian currency as a circulating medium. Southwestern states used Mexican pesos. In other areas local businessmen tried various substitutes and alternatives.[15]

The Goldmans' methods during this crisis illustrated the imagination and boldness which distinguished so much of their careers in business. Not long after establishing themselves in Oklahoma City, they concocted a sales-promotion project designed to appeal to a depression-conscious public. They purchased a series of coupon books in denominations of five, ten, and twenty dollars. Each book contained coupons with perforated divisions. Sections could be torn out to make change. Customers could purchase these coupon books each payday and use them to buy groceries until the next payday. Families wishing to ensure an adequate food supply but fearing to trust their willpower at budgeting found the coupons convenient. Those forced to leave their children with babysitters while they worked also appreciated the device, for coupons could be redeemed by anyone, but only for groceries at Standard stores.

The coupon books had already become an established part of the chain's policy when the bank holiday was announced in March, 1933. The Goldmans, following the lead of Oklahoma City's other chain operators, issued instructions to their store managers not to cash any checks until after the federal government reorganized the banking system. During the morning of the banks' closing, the president of Standard Food Markets received a telephone call from a store manager questioning the no-check dictum in light of a request to cash one from Sylvan's own wife. Humorous though the situation seemed, it caused the chain president to think about other Oklahoma City housewives in similar predicaments. He reversed his earlier decision and ordered all the store managers to cash checks offered by their regular customers for the amount of purchase and to exchange food coupon books for customers' payroll checks.

This judgment made, Goldman characteristically explored the situation for ways of turning it to his company's advantage. Realizing that workers all over the city had to be paid and that there was not enough currency in circulation to cash the checks, he proposed a unique plan to a number of businessmen and firms with whom he dealt. In lieu of meeting their payrolls with what were at that moment uncashable checks, Goldman offered to sell them coupon books to be distributed as part of their employees' salaries. The businessmen agreed, and hundreds of local workers received Standard coupons in their pay envelopes. An unexpected extension of the idea occurred when streetcar conductors were instructed to accept Standard coupons as well as cash for fares.

The executives of the Standard chain were pleased with the increased flow of shoppers in their stores. They could reasonably expect to retain some of these new customers as regular patrons when the crisis ended. There was only one drawback. Cashed checks, stored in vaults, finally reached such proportions that if they remained uncollected they would bankrupt the company. Although the store managers had been cautioned not to accept checks from strangers, several of them indicated to Goldman that they were suspicious of some checks. When the banks reopened during the second week in March, the Standard stores hurriedly deposited their accumulation of paper. More than half came back stamped "insufficient funds" or, more dismayingly, "no account." Putting aside his initial consternation, Goldman sent the returned checks to the stores that had taken them and attached special instructions concerning their collection. The writers of the checks were reached individually, while small signs in each store made the pointed observation, "We cashed your check when no one else did." Strategically posted near each checkout stand, the signs had the desired effect. Most customers quickly settled their debts, explaining that they had not yet been able to deposit funds to cover the checks written during the bank holiday; others admitted that they had no checking accounts and had been driven by desperation to write hot checks to get food for their families, but they promised that when they had a payday their debts to the stores would be among the first obligations they would meet.

Within a month every returned check except one had been redeemed. Ironically, it bore Sylvan Goldman's initialed approval. A man who was not a regular customer had come to the Standard office and asked for Goldman. When admitted to the office, he told Goldman that he wanted to give his check for twenty-five dollars for coupon books. Goldman had approved the transaction. The resulting loss was the only deficit incurred from a plan that had paid a handsome dividend of increased business and had brought Standard many future customers.[16]

The decade 1930 to 1940 was a difficult time for the Goldmans. They started with little capital and then underwent one of the country's greatest depressions. During that ten-year period the Oklahoma City area was a competitive market, especially in the chain-store food business. The Atlantic and Pacific Food Stores, the largest chain in the United States, waged a strong fight to obtain volume and, after operating there for some time, came out with signs on the fronts of their stores: "Prices Nailed Down to Stay Down." Their prices were low because of their buying ability. Yet because of the stiff competition, one Saturday night the chain's management suddenly closed all its twenty-one stores in the city and moved out of the area permanently.

In addition, Kroger Grocery Company, the third-largest chain in the United States, sold its stores and large warehouse to Safeway, which discontinued the Kroger name. Piggly Wiggly Stores were also sold, and the name was discontinued. Clarence Saunders, who originated Piggly Wiggly Stores, opened a new chain in Oklahoma City, along with others elsehwere in the country, and operated the stores under his name, but the new chain went bankrupt. Its member stores were purchased by investors, who changed the chain's name; later they too failed. In this ten-year span all these chains and a few smaller ones—a total of ten—moved out, sold, or went broke.

The Goldmans' business venture in Oklahoma City, begun in a depression atmosphere, could be accounted a solid success before the hard times disappeared at the coming of the World War II. What had started as a group enterprise eventually became Sylvan Goldman's sole responsibility. His three closest business associates, all members of the family, were no longer with the company, two of them because of tragic circumstances. Uncle Henry Dreyfus, the Goldmans' financial and business counselor, died under unusual conditions in 1935. A longtime horseback-riding enthusiast, Dreyfus broke his ankle as a result of a fall while indulging in his favorite sport. What should have been a minor incident turned into tragedy when a blood clot developed and subsequently caused his death.

Two years later Alfred Goldman, who had been closely associated with his brother from the start of their business career and had been a major influence in the operation of the business, took a vacation with his wife on a ship from Galveston, Texas, to New York. The trip was intended to be restful and relaxing, but in 1937 there were, of course, no

Alfred D. Goldman in 1937, just before his death (Goldman Collection).

ships with air conditioning, and on this trip the weather became very hot. The couple's stateroom had only ceiling fans for cooling, and Alfred caught a bad cold. Before they arrived in New York, the cold progressed into pneumonia, and he died in a hospital in New York the day after Sylvan flew to his bedside. Soon after the close of World War II, Morris Dreyfus, the Goldmans' bachelor uncle who had been supervisor of stores, retired from active participation in the company.[17] The death of his Uncle Henry Dreyfus and his brother Alfred and the retirement of Uncle Morris Dreyfus left Sylvan with an awesome and lonely responsibility. According to the terms of the family agreement, in the event of a partner's death the heirs would receive payment for the deceased's interest in the business plus his share of the profits during the year following his death. Goldman and Morris Dreyfus struggled to uphold this obligation to the estate of Henry Dreyfus and Alfred Goldman. Thus they had been unable to accumulate a large capital reserve by 1946, the year Morris Dreyfus retired. Morris, a bachelor, wanted to enjoy his life free of the operation and expansion of the business. His nephew thus found himself with the additional financial burden of acquiring Dreyfus' interest. The ten-year span from the late 1930's to the late 1940's therefore marked a time of continual stress for Goldman who had to contend with a lingering economic depression, family obligations, and government price regulations during the war and the postwar era. Goldman bought Morris Dreyfus' interest with cash and with notes for the balance to be paid from future profits.

Three decades later, in a rare period of reminiscing, Sylvan looked back on those personal trials:

> I was lucky when I first went to work in the wholesale grocery business because a man with a so-called million-dollar

smile first showed me the ropes. The influence on me by my uncle and business partner, Henry Dreyfus, was considerable. He was a man who had learned the food business from the proverbial ground up. An astute person, he had arrived in Tulsa during the early days of the oil boom. Starting in a small wholesale produce operation, he and his brothers were soon to expand the business to include groceries.

In the mid-1920's Henry Dreyfus foresaw the trend and development of chain stores to handle their own wholesale operations and to buy direct from processors. He was quick to organize a retail chain, and my brother Alfred and I were promptly charged with full responsibility of operation. His unexpected death when he was in the prime of his life was a great blow, for he was a close relative, friend and wise business counselor.

One of the main reasons for our success in our shaky new start in Oklahoma City following the stockmarket crash was the balancing influence of my brother Alfred. He was always reserved, far more than I. He had a quick, alert mind and a keen sense of humor. His sensitivity to the needs of both customers and employees created an unusually suitable background for the thriving buying, merchandising, and headquarters of our Tulsa Sun Stores chain. And, during the exhausting first seven years of our Standard–Humpty Dumpty history, he saw to it that many of the principles of doing business we observed were put into effect in the infancy of our business.

No two brothers could have worked more closely than we did. His characteristic patience and ability to listen before making a decision was the reason for his making and keeping many friends.

In 1930, when we decided to tackle Oklahoma City in spite of the thunderclouds of depression, Alfred and I formed a management team with our uncle Morris Dreyfus. After our years of association in Tulsa we thought alike, approached problems from the same viewpoint and shared the basic business philosophy of progress through service.

Morris was a bachelor, so long hours of work meant no more to him than it did to me. As Supervisor of Stores he was tireless, pitching in whenever and wherever he was needed. He gave me total support in developing the executive team we needed to achieve the ever-expanding needs of our rapid growth during the World War II years.

His warm smile, innate understanding of human relationships, and his soft-spoken words were the ingredients that led to his unusual capacity for getting along with people. It was Morris who made it a number one requirement for management, employees and the organization as a whole to supply every customer with complete shopping satisfaction.[18]

If Sylvan Goldman's achievements had been confined to just his part in building the Standard-Humpty Dumpty chain, his career would be reckoned notable. In addition to the extension of the chain during and after the war, he also was involved in other business ventures and in national and international food organizations, especially the Super Market Institute. Perhaps the phase of his career which earned Goldman his greatest renown was the one that began in the Depression era with an idea. The idea became an invention and the invention a symbol of the retail food industry everywhere in the world.

4. The Grocery Cart and Other Inventions

Life in the United States is characterized by a multitude of everyday devices whose origins have never been questioned and whose utility has rarely been remarked. Perhaps their constant presence has rendered them so ordinary that people simply overlook them. Among those items thrown off by the technological whirl of the 1930's was one that helped to revolutionize the retail grocery business and, in fact, became the symbol of the supermarket industry. Three of America's best known magazines—*Life*, *Look*, and the *Saturday Evening Post*—chose to feature the device on their covers to call attention to issues devoted to the retail food trade. Likewise, when cartoonists have sought to suggest the presence of their characters in grocery stores, this object has appeared in their drawings. It has been used in uncounted newspaper and magazine ads and television commercials. Now worldwide in its myriad uses and an omnipresent symbol of American ingenuity is Sylvan Goldman's invention—the shopping cart—which now has a customer-imposed identification as "The Cart That Changed the World."

An ordinary folding chair was the inspiration that spawned this device that helped revolutionize the retail grocery business. Goldman had long thought about how to expand the natural limits of a grocery shopper's purchases. His stores, like others of that era, had a supply of wicker or wire market baskets. These baskets became heavy as they were filled with food items, particularly for the woman buyer, who usually did most of the shopping. In an effort to offset this problem, Goldman had issued instructions that certain store personnel should keep a watchful eye for shoppers with loaded baskets and offer them empty ones to finish their buying. The filled baskets were to be taken to designated checkstands, where the customers could pick them up later. One evening in 1936, as he worked late in his office, his attention was drawn to two ordinary folding chairs there. With a sudden burst of insight, he envisioned a solution to the problem of the arm-weary shopper. If the seat of a folding chair was raised several inches and another similar seat added below, a basket could be placed on each of them. Wheels attached to each leg would make the chair mobile, and the back of the chair could be adapted as a handle to push the cart. The basic drudgery of grocery buying would be eliminated, and the volume of grocery sales would be greatly increased.

Excited about his idea, Goldman sent for Fred Young, a maintenance man and carpenter employed by the Standard–Humpty Dumpty chain. Goldman described his idea to Young, who took the chair to his worktable for the first of a long series of tinkering sessions. Finally, the initial model was ready for a trial run in Goldman's office. An insignificant wooden match lying on the floor provided the

Sylvan Goldman's nesting cart, made by the Folding Carrier Company, was the model for this *Life* magazine cover. The company's name and the cart serial number are faintly discernible on the base of the basket. Courtesy Time-Life, Inc.

LIFE

SPECIAL ISSUE

FOOD

MASS LUXURY:
A $73 BILLION
MARKET BASKET

20 CENTS

JANUARY 3, 1955

G. U. S. PAT. OFF.

first obstacle to the new invention. The cart not only failed to run over the match but also buckled and tried to fold when its forward motion was stopped. This problem was solved by moving the lower basket holder to an off-center position so that the folding motion would not begin when the cart was pushed into an object. Another problem to be solved before the invention could be introduced to the public was that the casters on the front part of the frame almost fell off as the cart was pushed over a curb. Young devised a better method of keeping the casters, as well as the rear supports, which were regular wheels, in place.[1] A year after the cart was put into use the baby seat was developed when it was seen that children were often placed in the baskets. Besides being dangerous, that practice made the basket ineffective for carrying groceries.

Nearly forty years later Goldman recalled the process by which the shopping cart had taken shape and gave Young a full share of the credit for providing the mechanical skills necessary to perform the task. "I'm no mechanic," Goldman stated. "I might be able to make a toothpick out of a piece of wood with a good sharp knife. But if you have a good imagination and can think of the idea, you can find someone to build it for you."[2]

The two men worked several months in this manner—Goldman suggesting innovations and improvements and Young applying them to a working model. Goldman wanted a steel-framed carrier, mounted on wheels, that would ac-

Goldman's earliest model shopping cart appears in this illustration on the August 31, 1940, cover of *The Saturday Evening Post*. Courtesy Saturday Evening Post.

commodate two shopping baskets. Accordingly, shelves were devised to hold wide-mesh metal baskets. The lower shelf was about nine inches from the floor with a twenty-inch clearance between it and the upper shelf. When open, the apparatus measured twenty-four inches in length, eighteen inches in width, and a little more than thirty-six inches in height. The rear wheels, which were made of rubber, accounted for four inches of that height, while the front swivel casters measured three inches in diameter. One of the invention's strong selling points was the small space it occupied when folded. After the baskets were removed from the seats, the folded cart took up a scant five inches of floor space. Perhaps the most impressive dimensions, from a grocery-store manager's viewpoint, were those of the steel-wire baskets. They measured nineteen inches long, thirteen inches wide, and nine inches deep. With their sloping sides they could be stacked in a nesting arrangement that took up very little space, an additional selling point.[3]

Goldman's folding carrier was not the first attempt to "come to grips with the problem that had to be solved before the modern supermarket could exist, the problem of a vehicle on which to carry one's purchases as he worked his way through the aisles."[4] John and Paul Cifrino, the founders of Upham's Corner Market in Boston, had been among the first to try to achieve a solution. In the early 1920's, they had evolved a system whereby their customers shopped from counter to counter, selecting groceries and receiving from clerks slips of paper designating the items they chose. The purchases were then transported to checkout stands by means of a conveyor belt. The customer had completed his shopping without having lifted anything heavier than the slips of paper with which he claimed his marketing choices. Unfortunately for the Cifrinos, their system suffered from two defects that proved impossible to overcome. First, the conveyor belt had a tendency to break down during rush hours, and, second, the system required a large number of clerks, a drawback that defeated the purpose of a self-service operation.[5]

Another effort bore a closer kinship to Goldman's contribution. Like many innovations in the retail food business, it grew out of the fierce competition among the industry's members. One of the earliest supermarket operations was the store of Henke and Pillot, in Houston, Texas. Pioneering in self-service stores in 1919, they had laid out a floor plan in the shape of an M. The shelving around the perimeter was stocked from the rear. A fifteen-inch-wide track, raised about thirty inches from the floor and fitted with low side-rails, ran along the shelves and carried baskets equipped with tiny wheels grooved to slide inside the rails. While this system eliminated the burden of carrying overladen baskets, it was not adaptable to stores with different floor plans. In addition, shoppers were forced to follow the entire track. This discouraged people who came in to buy a few items and had to wait behind slower customers.

J. Weingarten, Inc., the chief competitor of Henke and Pillot in Houston, had asked one of its employees to devise an answer to the stationary track. Ellis D. Turnham had met this challenge by removing the handle from a toy express wagon, making the front wheel stationary, and fitting the wagon bed with a basket so that the customer could pull it around by the basket handle. Later Turnham constructed a steel carrier that could be pushed, but it had no folding device and carried only one regular basket. There were only a few of these wagons in a store because they could not be folded or nested, and they took up too much valuable space.[6]

*"What I don't like about these self-service
stores is I'm always overselling myself."*

Courtesy Saturday Evening Post

These experiments, while intriguing in their possibilities, had failed to make an impression on the retail-food scene. Nor did they enjoy any use beyond the few stores in which they were originally employed in the chain. Goldman had no knowledge of these early attempts to devise a carrier (later his own design would be adopted by these Texas chains whose own efforts had failed in practical use). Goldman's invention provided an efficient and rapid means of streamlining the self-service concept. As long as shoppers were limited to buying only what they could physically carry in one basket, sales would be small. The dual baskets featured in the Goldman invention greatly increased the volume a customer could carry.

Once Goldman's invention had been perfected for practical use, it had to be "sold" to customers. This task proved nearly as difficult as originating and perfecting the concept. Goldman's invention had revealed an alert and imaginative mind; the manner in which he promoted his creation illustrated his talents as an entrepreneur and a merchandising specialist. On June 4, 1937, the inventor began advertising his new product with a flair that was typical of supermarket ballyhoo, but with an added titillation that showed Goldman's understanding of human nature. The advertisement featured a picture of a tired-looking woman clutching her purse in one hand and a heavily loaded market basket in the other. In bold type the caption beside the illustration read, "Basket Juggling Is a Lost Art at Your Standard Food Stores." The text accompanying the visual art emphasized "the newest innovation in shopping! Exclusive now at your Standard stores." The ad then described the joys of "wending your way through a spacious food market without having to carry a cumbersome shopping basket on your arm. . . . Just pick your items from the

Newspaper ads hinting at the shopping-cart innovation, Oklahoma City, 1937.

shelves. They will be checked and placed in your car without having to carry a single item." This rhetoric was distinguished by its flamboyant "hard-sell" flavor, as well as by a careful omission of any specific information concerning the device that was to transform shopping from drudgery to ecstasy. Goldman had cleverly touted his product without mentioning its name, thus piquing the curiosity of his readers.[7]

One week later he repeated the same format in another newspaper advertisement, which announced that "Standard's new 'No Basket Carrying Plan' met with instant approval last week-end." Again, there was no descriptive mention of the miraculous wonder.[8] From the tenor of the copy shoppers might have assumed that the folding basket carrier was an instant success, but the reverse was true. Goldman, confident of a ready and enthusiastic customer response, had positioned a young woman inside the turnstiles to offer the entering shoppers the use of one of the carts with the two baskets on it. The young woman was nonplused and her employer chagrined when both men and women coming into the store refused to use the new carriers.

In his 1977 interview with Charles Kuralt, Goldman recalled his reaction to seeing customers reject the shopping cart:

> I got down to the store about 10 o'clock in the morning waiting for the time when people'll start coming in, and this was right on a . . . Saturday when it's your biggest day, and I knew that I'd be seeing people lined up at the door to get in to get the merchandise and see what the dickens it was. And when I got there, I went to our largest store, there wasn't a soul using a basket carrier, and we had an attractive girl by the entrance that had a basket carrier and two baskets in it, one on the top and one on the bottom, and asked them to please take

this cart to do their shopping with. And the housewives, most of 'em decided, "No more carts for me. I have been pushing enough baby carriages. I don't want to push anymore." And the man would say, "You mean, with my big strong arm that I can't carry a darn little basket like that?" And he wouldn't touch it. It was a complete flop.

The only people who accepted the shopping innovation at all were the elderly.

Over the weekend Goldman considered how to get public acceptance of his carriers, whose utility he did not doubt. "Wednesday evening it happened to dawn on me—an idea—and we put that into effect." His goal was "to show that the carts weren't wheeled monsters." His plan was simple but effective:

> I hired for each store a young lady about in her late twenties, another lady in her forties, and someone else about in their late fifties, and I hired a couple of men about thirty years old and about fifty years old and they were in the store with basket carriers shopping, pushing the cart around. They had merchandise in the top basket, and bottom basket. These people were shopping right by the entranceway of the store.

Here Charles Kuralt interrupted Goldman to ask, "Shills?"

Goldman replied:

> That's right. Exactly what it was. So, I told this young lady that was offering the carts to the customer to say, "Look, everybody's using them; why not you?" And when they saw them in use, they started using them, and immediately it became a huge success. All because of the fact that somebody else had to get the ball rolling.

Within a few weeks all the Standard and Humpty Dumpty stores in Goldman's chain were using the folding carriers, and they were a huge success.[9]

At the start Young, with the aid of one assistant and a

high school youth who worked after school, produced the carriers in a sheet-metal carpenter's shed that measured twenty by fifty feet. The shed was situated beyond the Standard-Humpty Dumpty main office building. Their equipment consisted of a secondhand punch press, a spot welder, and a few other tools. At first they constructed only enough carts to supply the Standard and Humpty Dumpty stores. The first grocery market outside the firm to buy the carriers was a chain in Amarillo, Texas, whose owner saw the carts in use in Oklahoma City.

The history of the spread of the invention, beginning with this purchase, might have been different had Goldman not received an interesting piece of mail in August, 1937. A notice informed him of plans for the special Super Market Institute to be held in New York City. Among the features of this first meeting of the nation's supermarket operators was a large series of exhibits displaying food products and grocery-store equipment. Goldman saw this meeting as an opportunity to publicize and demonstrate his carrier to the people who would be most interested in it—store owners. Goldman decided to display the product of his Folding Basket Carrier Company, which by now he had organized and incorporated, at the convention's exhibits, but the recent death of his brother made him reluctant to leave Oklahoma City to handle the arrangements himself. Therefore, he wrote Kurt Schweitzer, a cousin by marriage who owned an import-export business in New York, to ask him to find a man to set up and manage an exhibit booth. Schweitzer had trouble finding a good man for the task, which fell on a weekend, so he agreed to do the job himself. As events unfolded, Goldman was able to attend the meeting, and he helped Schweitzer organize the Folding Basket Carrier booth. The interest and enthusiasm which the dis-

Goldman's first folding basket carrier was made in this building. A number of the carriers were manufactured here between 1937 and 1938. (Goldman Collection)

play attracted led Schweitzer to approach Goldman with a proposition. If Goldman would give him a commission on sales east of the Mississippi, Schweitzer would quit his own business and work full time selling carts in that part of the United States. The two men agreed to this arrangement, and Goldman left for Oklahoma immediately after the convention.

Schweitzer and his wife, Hortense, also headed west a few weeks later. They took a circuitous route, stopping at chain grocery stores and independent markets in major cities between New York and St. Louis, Missouri. From there they drove directly to Oklahoma City to tell Goldman

The original Folding Carrier Building after remodeling. (Goldman Collection)

what they had experienced while demonstrating and trying to sell the carriers. They had expected to write orders in large quantities, but they arrived at Goldman's home very discouraged. Only a few store operators had placed orders, and these were in small quantities to test the Oklahoma groceryman's invention. They had expressed fears that the shoppers' children would regard the carts as playthings and race them up and down the aisles, knocking merchandise off shelves and into customers, causing injuries. Lawsuits might ensue from cart-related accidents, the storekeepers said, and thus the carriers' possible utility simply did not warrant the risks involved.

Goldman had not encountered these problems in his Oklahoma City stores, and he gave considerable thought to the best method of convincing others of the carts' utility and safety. In 1977 he explained to Kuralt how he solved the problem.

> We took one of our stores after closing hours and we took a group of our employees and had them act as customers shopping, and some of them, of course, were the employees in the store, and we took a movie and showed exactly how this worked in the stores and how easily and how well it was accepted, and the problems a lot of them were thinking about didn't show up at all, and how the customers were buying so much more merchandise because the two baskets became full.
>
> After the film was finished, I told Kurt Schweitzer, "Now when you go in to try to see the fixture buyer, tell him—if they ask you what you're selling—tell 'em you have something new and the only thing you can do is show it to them." And what he did was take his projector in with the film, shut off the light, close the door, and show it on a wall. You don't need a screen for doing it. And he showed these pictures on the wall, and they would bring in some of their top executives to look at it; before he got halfway back to New York, we had so many orders for carts, we couldn't have made them in God knows how long a time.

With this basic merchandising technique established, orders for carts arrived in Oklahoma City from various parts of the country. It quickly became apparent that the Folding Basket Carrier Company would have to expand to take care of the increased volume. As business came in, the plant had to be enlarged materially and new, modern equipment purchased. Unable to spare time from directing his grocery chain, Goldman relied on A. K. Weiss to handle the home office, while Schweitzer was in charge of sales for his territory—and he was a supersalesman.[10]

In 1939, because of the problem of maneuvering loaded baskets from the carrier and sacking groceries with the least wasted motion, Goldman fashioned a completely new checkout system for his stores. Normally, a market manager had his cash registers on waist-high counters at the front of the store. Before the introduction of shopping carts, customers would place their baskets on the counter for the clerk to empty item by item while ringing up prices on his register. If business was brisk, a sacker would put the groceries from the counter into paper sacks. Goldman's revised checkout system was suggested for clerks who had to reach across the loading counter which was from two to three feet wide, to lift baskets off the carrier.

The Folding Carrier Company's advertising contained instructions and diagrams explaining how to renovate a store's checkout system to accommodate the double-decker carriers. According to the diagrams, an L-shaped counter would serve best. The right angle of the L faced the customer as he pushed his cart up to it. On the corner of the angle rested the cash register, its sides forming parallel lines running diagonally from the corner. Immediately to the storefront side of the register, a square space was cut out of the counter's interior. Six inches of counter space separated this cutout from a larger, diagonally cut section three feet across. The shopper's loaded carrier was to be pushed into this larger slot and unloaded by the store checker with his left hand while he used his right to tally the items on the register. As he lifted the groceries from the basket, he would pack them in an already opened sack resting on and being supported by Goldman's newest gadget, the grocery sacker. This ingenious-but-simple device—a three-sided metal wire stand, approximately three feet high, with a shelf built into the frame eighteen inches from its top—

This cutout space in the checkstand allowed the checker to ring up items as she removed them from the basket and load them into a grocery sack that was held upright by a wire rack. Both the cutout and the wire rack were developed by Goldman. (Goldman Collection)

stood in the counter cutout between the shopping cart slot and the cash register.[11]

Although the grocery sacker eliminated the need for an additional worker at the checkstand, the innovation did not become popular at that time because too many merchants were reluctant to cut a piece out of their checkstands. But today most checkstands are separated so that clerks can check items from the basket as intended by this invention. Goldman was convinced of the sacker's worth and was surprised by the scant enthusiasm accorded his checkout counter aid, on which the United States Patent Office awarded him six patentable claims. The cutout checkstand, however, caught the notice of many store owners and managers, who followed Goldman's suggestions or devised similar plans adapted to the use of his shopping carts. Later, of course, electrically powered belts were used to carry the grocery items along the counters.

Before designing the grocery sacker in 1939, Goldman had already marketed another product as a result of his continuous study of the developing supermarket. He had noticed that one of the most laborious tasks in any store was the stocking of shelves with groceries. Although various wheeled vehicles were used for transporting cartons and boxes from the storeroom, Goldman discovered an important improvement and produced his own store service truck. Constructed of heavy-duty steel and measuring sixteen by thirty-six inches, the bottom support frame could hold up to five hundred pounds of merchandise, normally about six to eight cases of canned goods. Rolling on ball-bearing wheels and casters, the truck load was steadied from front and rear by steel frames. One of the unique features of the truck was its hinged top rack, which was brought over the top of the front upright frame to latch onto the back frame. Cases of cans or other items were placed on this rack, eliminating the need to stoop to empty the contents of the box when the upper shelves were being stocked. This simple innovation speeded the time-consuming task of restocking. In the beginning it was turned over to Schweitzer to merchandise only in his territory. It quickly became a fast-selling item throughout the industry and still sells in volume to food stores, although it has undergone very few changes from its original design.[12]

Another Folding Carrier product that found an appreciative public was a natural offshoot of the shopping carrier. If grocery buying was made easier because of a cart, then a similar conveyance might be useful in other businesses that required the handling of many articles. By 1940, Goldman's firm was filling orders for his Folding Inter-Office Basket Carrier. Designed for office use, these carriers rapidly became popular with office workers who handled large numbers of files, books, and mail. They closely resembled the shopping cart in construction, and they possessed the usual folding feature for storage. The baskets measured fourteen inches by twenty inches by eight and one-half inches deep. Among the buyers of the carriers were the DuPont Company, offices of the United States Senate, the United States Navy Supply Division, and many grateful librarians.[13]

Once launched in the manufacturing of metal baskets, Goldman continually discovered new applications for them in his grocery stores. The familiar olive green painted metal that had become synonymous with Folding Carrier products provided the structural material for two types of merchandise holders. The National Biscuit Company, processor of crackers and cookies, was the biggest purchaser of Goldman's floor display stands. These devices were light-

STORE SERVICE TRUCK
Folding Basket Carrier Co.
20 N. Douglas St.
Okla City, Okla

Goldman invented this store service truck that eliminated bending over to reach each item when stocking the shelves. It was manufactured and sold by Folding Carrier Company. (Goldman Collection).

weight, wire-framed stands especially suited to displaying cellophane-wrapped foods. Taking up less than four square feet of floor space, the three-tiered stands could be placed virtually anywhere in a store.[14] Gerber Products Company of Fremont, Michigan, used another Folding Carrier Company wire display in the late 1940's to experiment—successfully—with customer psychology. Gerber's main sales item, baby food, could be displayed advantageously in three- and five-dozen-jar baskets. Gerber executives believed that a jumbled array of baby food would increase sales, because it would be easier for customers to take the small items from baskets than from closely stacked shelves.[15]

Goldman also turned his eye on his grocery stores' dairy cases. The result was still another merchandising innovation that proved as popular with dairy companies as with retail grocers. In the 1930's, an era of glass milk bottles and completely closed cooling storage cases, the biggest problem of both retailers and milk suppliers was keeping the product fresh while displaying it. Loaded from the front, milk displays represented a special problem in restocking. Careless or lazy milk deliverers tended to leave the bottles on hand at the rear of the case and to put the fresh milk bottles in the front empty spaces. As a result of this practice, sour milk was often sold. Goldman eliminated this problem by placing the bottles in appropriately sized metal holders. There were two models of the patented Handy Milk Bottle Racks. One kind consisted of a slanted slide rack in which gravity forced the rear bottles forward as customers removed the one in front. In the second design a spring holder drew the rear bottles forward on a flat surface as the front ones were removed. The bases on both models were made of galvanized steel, as was the spring on the second type, while the bottles were held in line on the sides by steel wire. Quart, pint, and half-pint bottles could be accommodated by different-sized holders. Restocking was done from the rear, and it was so easy that the deliverymen were less inclined to stock carelessly. They had only to fill in the empty spaces in the back of the rack. *Popular Mechanics* magazine and a trade journal, *Dairy World*, published articles, with pictures and text, about Goldman's invention. Both models of racks sold well until the advent of waxed milk cartons and open refrigerated display cases.[16]

World War II greatly affected the Folding Carrier Company, just as it changed or modified the direction of most American business activity. A. K. Weiss went into the army in World War II. Kurt Schweitzer was prevailed upon to come to Oklahoma City as president and general manager of Folding Carrier Company in charge of sales and expansion. Goldman and Schweitzer dealt with a wartime shortage of materials, a dwindling labor supply, and the necessity of retooling for war production. Metal became a scarce commodity as the United States began turning out guns, ships, airplanes, and weapons. As a manufacturer of shopping carts, baskets, and grocery service trucks, Folding Carrier could not expect—and did not receive—a high ranking on the metals priority list except for those items needed in government commissaries in the United States and in foreign countries. By 1942 the company's advertising was carrying pictures and descriptions promoting wooden-doweled baskets and wooden carriers. The only metal used in the otherwise oak construction was in the frame fastenings.

Wood also was used in manufacturing ration-stamp change boxes, yet another of Goldman's inventions. During the war the government ordered meat-market operators to give change for purchases with red stamps in denominations of one, two, five, and six points. Goldman's little device, less than nine inches long, proved very popular with harassed butchers who had to handle the flimsy stamps.[17]

Before Pearl Harbor brought the nation to war, the armed forces sought out manufacturing plants that could be converted for war production. In December, 1940, the Navy Ordnance Department requested complete, detailed information on Folding Carrier's facilities and capabilities. The plant had been inspected by navy personnel in August, a visit that made it probable that the navy would use the Oklahoma City plant. On December 8, 1941, the day after the Japanese attack, Weiss received a warning from the navy suggesting that precautions be taken to prevent sabotage of the factory's facilities.[18]

The war was less than a month old when Folding Carrier received its first war contract. The basket-carrier assembly line was to manufacture tiny arming wire assemblies for one-thousand-pound bombs. According to the terms of the contract more than a hundred thousand of the small but essential components were to be manufactured. Company employees were made to feel the importance of their task by periodic checks by federal officers for quality, safety, and security. Lieutenant General Leonard H. Campbell, Jr., chief of ordnance for the navy, later wrote a special letter of commendation for the retooling efforts successfully accomplished by the Folding Carrier Company during the war.[19]

After the war Folding Carrier continued to grow and prosper. In 1950, Goldman purchased a 150,000-square-foot building to replace the plant that had housed the as-

When the Folding Carrier Company went into mass production, it moved into this building. (Goldman Collection)

sembly line, and operations were moved to the six-story structure to provide the necessary extended production space to meet a renewed demand for shopping carts and other products. This was one of four expansions carried out by the company. Schweitzer moved the headquarters office to the new location and, working closely with R. G. "Bud" Hammerhead, of the manufacturing department, did an outstanding job. Until his death Schweitzer continued to make the Folding Carrier Company a very successful operation.

Kurt Schweitzer poses with the Folding Carrier Company's 100,000th nesting cart. The cart, still in Goldman's possession, has been bronzed. (Goldman Collection)

The new plant was equipped with a complete chrome-plating apparatus, the only one in Oklahoma. The firm's metal products no longer exhibited the olive-green color that had marked them since the 1930's.[20] But more than the color was changed in the company's major line of merchandise, the shopping cart. In 1947, Folding Carrier introduced the patented Nest Kart. The new cart enabled grocers to store one-piece carriers in a smaller area than that required by the older models with their removable baskets. The back section of the carrier basket, now an integral part of the frame, swung forward when the front of a second carrier was pushed against it, allowing any number of carts to nest, each partly enclosing the one behind it. The 1950 model had a basket with a capacity of 5,600 cubic inches, plus a lower-front slanting shelf for large purchases. Tubular, one-piece frame construction with a chrome finish gave the cart a more streamlined appearance than that of the older models.[21]

Another important feature of the nesting carts was the built-in baby seat. Constructed of a closer-meshed wire, the baby seat accommodated children with a hinged plate that could be dropped from the upper portion of the rear end of the basket, exposing a divided opening through which the child's legs fit. When marketing the original folding carrier, Goldman had not foreseen that the cart's biggest attraction would be its baby-sitting potentialities, but harried mothers were glad to have both hands free for shopping while their young children were safe in the upper basket. Generations of women have gratefully used the baby seats since 1940.

Not all customers appreciated this feature of Goldman's invention, however. In July, 1942, newspaper readers in Dallas, Texas, were surprised to discover that a complaining motion had been placed before the city manager to prohibit putting children or pets in grocery carts while shopping. Ostensibly, the babies' wet diapers caused the baskets to be insanitary for the next customer. A storm of protest greeted the Dallas Health Department when it ruled in favor of the complainant. No other city cared to follow the Dallas health officials' action after aroused mothers accused them of being "heartless, selfish child-haters" and "narrow-minded, thoughtless politicians." Luckily, the entire episode subsided peacefully; no ordinance was passed.[22]

To take care of toddlers, the Nest Kart Junior was marketed in 1952. A miniature version of the regular-sized carrier, the junior cart was tested in stores in California and Oklahoma. A toy was placed in each cart. The toys kept the children occupied, and the parents almost invariably bought them. Four out of ten mothers left the stores after purchasing two complete carts full of food, many of the items selected by the children, who proved to be as susceptible to impulse buying as adults.[23]

There seemed to be no end to the refinements that could be made to enhance the practicality of grocery carts. Folding Carrier experimented with various designs and basket sizes, trying to reach as large a market as possible. Goldman's model of 1939 offered an optional advertising plate built into the upright handle over the basket. Although the carriers of 1952 could be similarly equipped, the con-

Folding Carrier Company began marketing Nest Kart, Jr., in 1952, along with the regular-sized Nest Kart with baby seat. (Goldman Collection)

cept was never widely adopted. Grocers regarded the extra price as superfluous, because manufacturers did not reimburse the stores for advertising their products. In 1974, *Business Week* erroneously reported the shopping-cart advertisements' "first big test in 1,050 supermarkets in New England and upstate New York." An accompanying picture revealed a close resemblance between the so-called "new" device and Goldman's model of the 1930's. The success of the "innovation" came from a close working agreement with manufacturers.[24] Improved construction, including rubber bumpers and more efficient wheels and casters, helped keep Folding Carrier ahead of the rest of the industry and resulted in a steady growth for the Oklahoma City plant's sales, as well as for those of its Canadian subsidiary in Toronto.[25]

Constant attention to improvements in constructing and marketing the shopping carts was necessary if Folding Carrier was to maintain its lead in manufacturing and sales. At one time in the late 1930's the Oklahoma firm produced more than 70 percent of the national output. However, a number of competitors entered the field with slightly different carts, a relatively simple thing to do since Goldman's patents were rather easily evaded. Periodically conflicts developed over later Goldman patent claims and other applicants' inventions. Goldman's new-model nesting cart met with some difficulty. Arguments were presented in the patent hearings that this invention was not original; the dump truck and a type of cattle feeder supposedly operated on the same principle. However, Goldman's attorneys presented sufficient evidence to the contrary that an appeals judge was convinced and he ruled in their client's favor.[26] Another incident, in 1949, involved a lengthy appeal with Telescopic Carts of Kansas City, Missouri. The case ended in an out-of-court settlement.[27]

Another use of the cart came in the travel industry. At the request of the Santa Fe Railroad, headquartered in Topeka, Kansas, the Folding Carrier Company developed a luggage cart. After considerable design and construction research a prototype was sent to Topeka for a trial demonstration. The cart was to be used by passengers who traveled in chair cars and had no one to help them with their luggage (the redcaps served only the Pullman travelers). It was offered to chair-car passengers for use in transporting luggage to train platforms, loading docks, and exits at no charge. When customer reaction proved favorable in Topeka, the carts were placed in several other Santa Fe stations. They were extremely successful, and Folding Carrier Company received many orders from Santa Fe. Anticipating still larger orders, the company began manufacturing carts in advance for quick delivery. When the carriers were installed in the Santa Fe station in Chicago, however, redcap baggage handlers went on strike. The Santa Fe Company decided not to use the Goldman products, fearing a larger-scale strike. As a result the firm had no customers for the carts they had on hand.[28]

Left with a sizable number of carts that were apparently unmarketable, Goldman turned to another form of transportation as a possible outlet. He went to the Oklahoma City airport and persuaded the manager to accept a dozen free carts to see if the customers would use them to handle their luggage. Similar to the grocery carts, minus the large baskets, they contained space for two or three suitcases and included the baby seat made famous on grocery carts. Six-inch front wheels and eight-inch rear wheels gave the new product an outdoor utility and excellent mobility. Salesmen then called on other airports, and soon the Airport Personal Luggage Cart became a familiar item both in the United States and abroad.

An additional customer was discovered by Goldman when, returning from a trip abroad, he and his wife experienced difficulty in handling their luggage while going through customs, since no outside help was allowed until after the customs inspection. Goldman approached the customs office with the idea of equipping its departments with luggage carts. Before long most customs areas in the United States and many foreign countries were equipped with the luggage carriers.

In August, 1961, after his patents had run out, Goldman sold the Folding Carrier Company to Henry Litvak, a Chicago financier. The following year the company was acquired by Union Asbestos and Rubber Company of Chicago, now publicly owned and listed on the New York Stock Exchange as UNARCO Industries, Inc. Folding Carrier's 750 employees, including those with the Canadian operation, and its management staff, were not substantially changed in the transfer of company ownership.[29] Gene von Stein was the late Kurt Schweitzer's assistant, past vice-president of UNARCO Industries, Inc., and General Manager of its Folding Carrier Corporation subsidiary in Oklahoma City.

Although Goldman modestly maintains that if he had not invented the shopping cart someone else would have, Gene von Stein does not necessarily agree:

> Goldman's invention of the shopping cart was not just a "right place at the right time" happening. It was the result of continuing thought by an innovative man to solve an important problem in his stores. He did that, and simultaneously created, in my opinion, the greatest development in the history of merchandising. It was not a dormant idea awaiting someone to discover it. It truly has revolutionized worldwide retail distribution including both grocery supermarket and mass general merchandise store operations.

Another of Goldman's inventions was the luggage cart, manufactured and sold by Folding Carrier Company. First used by passenger trains, it is now used in most large airports all over the world. (Goldman Collection)

INTERNATIONAL

Herald Tribune

Published with The New York Times and The Washington Post

* *

PARIS, WEDNESDAY, OCTOBER 8, 1975

'Women customers would come in, and we had a young lady

with some carts with two baskets on them to

present to them for use, but very few would take one.'

Sylvan Goldman and How He Changed U.S. Life

By Lawrence Van Gelder

NEW YORK (NYT).—Everybody knows about Henry Ford and the Wright Brothers. But what about Sylvan Goldman?

Nearing his 76th birthday, he lives, as far as most Americans are concerned, in virtual anonymity. Yet there breathes scarcely an American, young or old, who at one time or another hasn't gotten behind the wheels of—or ridden in—his foremost invention. Life would not be the same without it.

grills, or remaining behind in the transformed and troubled cities.

Nobody knows how many shopping carts are rolling around in the United States but Safeway Stores, the country's largest supermarket chain, with more than 2,000 stores, says it bought 40,000 carts last year, at a cost of $2 million.

Another giant in the field, the A & P says that it buys 40,000 a year, at a cost of $2 million.

On the average, Safeway says, there are 150 carts to a store. They are expected to last about 10 years; during that time they

a clerk would see a customer's basket practically full, he would hand them another basket and tell them they could find their first basket of groceries by a certain checkout stand. Most always they would take this extra basket and keep shopping.

Goldman wrote: "In my office I had some folding chairs that the salesmen used when they called on me. I had the thought one day that if I would put wheels on the bottom of these folding chairs, raise the seats some so I could have room to put another rack at the bottom of the chair so this bottom rack could hold another

From its humble Depression-era beginnings in a carpentry shop in Oklahoma City, the shopping cart—like the automobile—has become big business.

Like the automobile, it is the centerpiece of competition for a multi-million-dollar market among the industry's big four, who send a million units a year (list price $30 to $70) down their assembly lines and off to the supermarkets to sing their silent subliminal siren song whose sole lyric is: Buy, buy.

In the nearly 40 years since the first Americans reluctantly went down the aisle for butter or wurst, in an uneasy marriage of convenience with Goldman's equivalent of the Model T, shopping carts have evolved—from a removable basket carried in something resembling a folding chair on wheels (the Smithsonian Institution has an original in its collection), to a computer-designed, chromed-steel answer to the Cadillac that starts at the touch of a fingertip and is intended to lure the shopper into bringing home a good deal more than just the bacon.

And while automobiles were flirting clumsily with aerodynamics and lengthening their fenders and sprouting portholes, shopping carts were being remodeled to eliminate the removability of the baskets, were growing tapered snouts and were learning to save space by nesting within one another.

In their ubiquitous but unremarkable way, they have rolled along with U.S. social history—rising out of the Depression, meeting the postwar baby boom with the folding baby seat, joining the exodus to the suburbs, there to gleam, be crushed or roll amok in shopping center parking lots or to be perverted into serving as barbecue

jected to maintenance. And, during that time, the wheels will be replaced about three times.

But to discuss the number of carts in terms of the more than 30,000 supermarkets (with at least $1 million in gross sales) in the country is to ignore the carts rolling around in smaller groceries, discount department stores (6,500 of them, with about 150 carts each) and in drug, liquor, garden supply and other stores where they have proved themselves useful to shoppers and store owners alike. And it ignores those vehicles that have been cartnapped to do duty in laundry rooms, offices and backyards.

Some carts have lasted for 20 years. They are, indeed, sturdy vehicles. According to some experts, they can support a dead weight of about 1,000 pounds—a structural strength mainly intended to help them to withstand the rigors of parking lots, where they hit and are hit, and are occasionally crushed by a truck.

The problem of how to enable shoppers to buy more in self-service groceries was one that led Goldman to come up with his invention.

"I used to own two chains of grocery stores—Standard Food Markets and Humpty Dumply Stores," Goldman wrote a few years ago in a letter addressed to the Department of Cultural History at the Smithsonian Institution. "In watching customers carrying baskets on their arms shopping for groceries, the thought came to me if there were some way we could give that customer two baskets to shop with and still have one hand free to shop we could do considerably more business, because usually when the housewife got her basket full it was heavy for her to carry and she would stop shopping. "On weekends we put some shopping baskets in the rear of our stores and when

of the chair be the handle of the basket carrier, this could be shopping in ease with two baskets. Then when the carts and baskets were not in use the carts could be folded and would not take up any more room than a folding chair, and the baskets of course were of the nesting type. This would give us ample room to store these carts and baskets in the front of the store, and keep a few carts open with baskets on them for customers to take and use."

And so, in his stores' carpentry shop at 20 North Douglas Street in Oklahoma City the shopping cart was born, and for all practical purposes made its debut in Goldman's stores in 1937.

And did the United States respond to the future with huzzahs? Certainly not.

Wrote Goldman: "Women customers would come in, and we had a young lady with some carts with two baskets on them to present to them for use, but very, very few would take one. Their comment was: No, we have pushed enough baby buggies around—we are not going to push carts in stores,' and the men customers would say. 'With my big arms I can carry my baskets, I am not pushing one of those things.' "

With the aid of hired help posing as customers using the carts and with the aid of motion pictures, Goldman was able to sell the idea of using the carts to his customers and sell the carts themselves, for $6 or $7, to other store owners, whose fear of accidents was overcome by watching his movies.

Looking back on it all the other day, Goldman, a prominent Oklahoman whose interests are now concentrated in real estate, spoke with a mixture of pride and modesty about the invention that changed life in the United States.

"It made a world of difference," he said. But, he added, "If it hadn't been me, somebody else would have invented it."

The concept for stores today, ever larger and often multi-purpose, was developed around the shopping cart. Without it they would not exist. It is the one piece of merchandise distribution equipment that has done more than any other to reduce labor costs and stimulate sales around the world, with truly profound effects in an historical sense on the way of life of hundreds of millions of people.

In 1938 a store owner in Texas called Goldman's shopping cart "the greatest asset to self-service grocery stores that has ever happened." [30] Certainly this praise was not an overstatement. This became apparent the next year when the Institute of American Inventors extended membership to Sylvan N. Goldman.[31] The Smithsonian Institution, Washington, D.C., acquired Goldman's original cart prototype. C. Malcolm Watkins, chairman of cultural history at the Smithsonian Institution, said of the acquisition:

> The folding carrier with baskets, the product of your invention and the prototype of the shopping cart that now plays such a universal role in the daily lives of Americans, is another "first" and unique addition to the national collections. We thank you for presenting to us this significant example of American ingenuity.

These official recognitions have ensured Goldman's place among American inventors. However, the actual worth of his contributions is better illustrated by its wide and varied uses. In 1972 nationally syndicated columnist Alice Widener wrote about a visit to Oklahoma City:

> I dined with the kind of American that collectivist-minded eggheads in the National Education Association said was extinct in our century. During the Great Depression they wrote "The day of the successful lone ranger in America is dead." Had that been true, America would have been dead. Happily, it wasn't. Our dinner host, Sylvan Goldman, is living proof of it. He is a onetime grocer who—as he puts it—"just had a simple

Courtesy Family Circle

idea." Others call it an invention. The simple idea was the shopping cart. Today, when you push around a shopping cart, be grateful to the silver-haired Oklahoma City grocer.

Later in her column Miss Widener referred to a visit to the Smithsonian Institution, where, she noted, the exhibits ranged from Goldman's original shopping cart to a piece of scintillating rock brought home from the moon by American astronauts.

To an optimist like Goldman this could be a veiled prediction: "Today the world, tomorrow the universe."

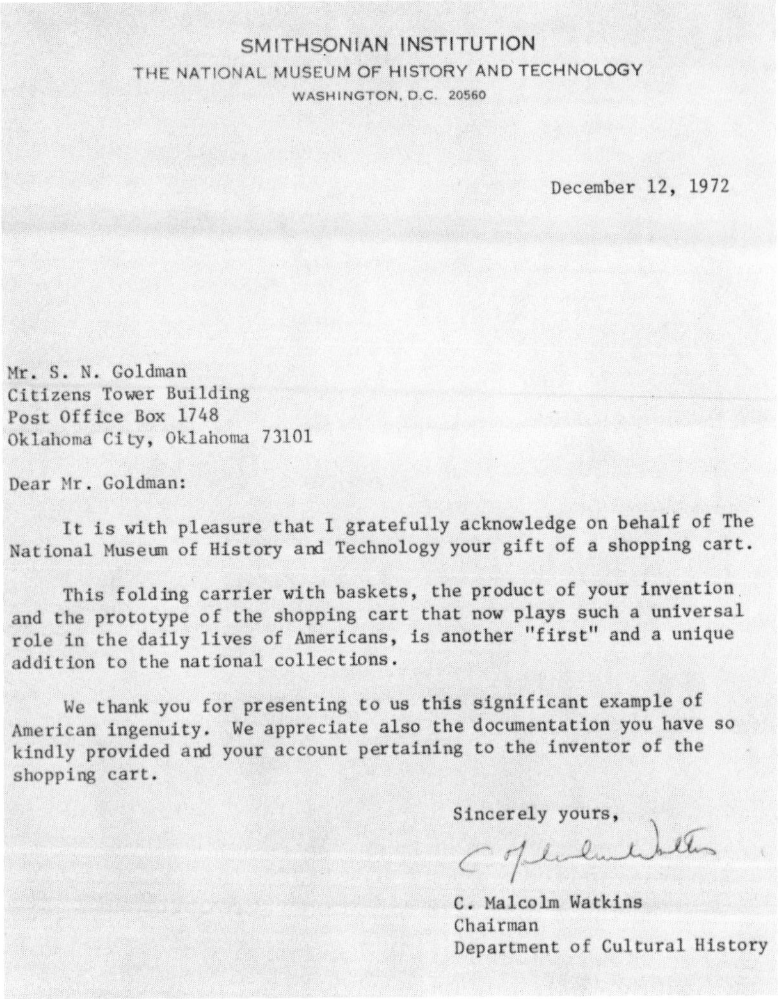

SMITHSONIAN INSTITUTION
THE NATIONAL MUSEUM OF HISTORY AND TECHNOLOGY
WASHINGTON, D.C. 20560

December 12, 1972

Mr. S. N. Goldman
Citizens Tower Building
Post Office Box 1748
Oklahoma City, Oklahoma 73101

Dear Mr. Goldman:

It is with pleasure that I gratefully acknowledge on behalf of The National Museum of History and Technology your gift of a shopping cart.

This folding carrier with baskets, the product of your invention and the prototype of the shopping cart that now plays such a universal role in the daily lives of Americans, is another "first" and a unique addition to the national collections.

We thank you for presenting to us this significant example of American ingenuity. We appreciate also the documentation you have so kindly provided and your account pertaining to the inventor of the shopping cart.

Sincerely yours,

C. Malcolm Watkins
Chairman
Department of Cultural History

A letter of appreciation from the Smithsonian Institution acknowledges Goldman's donation of the first grocery shopping cart. (Goldman Collection)

THE FOLDING BASKET
CARRIER COMPANY
20 NORTH DOUGLAS
OKLAHOMA CITY, OKLA.

THE FIRST
GROCERY SHOPPING CART

GRIN AND BEAR IT

BY LICHTY

"We're taking the grocery cart back to the
supermarket today . . . Junior is old enough to walk
now!"

Courtesy Field Newspaper Syndicate, Inc.

That the average citizen appreciated the shopping cart was perhaps shown most graphically by the passage of a city ordinance in Los Angeles making the "borrowing" of shopping carts from supermarkets punishable by a fine of five hundred dollars.[32] Federal Reserve Banks have used the carts to transfer coins and currency in their vaults, while Siphya Store, in Bangkok, Thailand, an import-export firm, uses "shopping wagons or vans ordered from your esteemed (Folding Carrier) company."[33] At this point in the twentieth century the carts are symbols of the self-service industry.

5. The Period of Rapid Revolution

As busy as he was with his inventions, Sylvan Goldman did not neglect his grocery chains. Much of the inventor's success could be measured by the extent to which he delegated responsibility for his burgeoning business enterprises, thus freeing himself to direct them all without becoming hopelessly mired in the day-to-day operation of any single one.

Kurt Schweitzer, as president and general manager, did an outstanding job of handling the Folding Carrier Company's sales and expansion during the 1940's. Before his death in 1960, he had opened branches in other areas and an assembly plant and sales office in Toronto, Canada. His wife, Hortense, was of great help to him, for she was equally well known in the industry. During this period Goldman's energies were aimed primarily at enlarging and extending the Standard–Humpty Dumpty chain, but his dual role of inventor and entrepreneur did not prevent him from assuming a major part in the establishment of the Super Market Institute. This organization recognized his formative contributions to the revolution in the food industry by electing him president and choosing his shopping cart as the symbol of the organization.

World War II and its resultant shortage of newsprint had forced Goldman to combine advertising for Standard and Humpty Dumpty stores. Although the stores continued as separate corporate entities, many of their functions and all of their executive control came from one source. Yet expansion went forward under the Humpty Dumpty name only. The first out-of-town store bearing the younger chain's designation was opened in Lawton, Oklahoma, in 1940; it was the ninth Humpty Dumpty store. Others followed in quick succession as Goldman set the pace for growth of supermarkets in the state. Before the war ended he had stores in Duncan, Bethany, Ada, Norman, and Midwest City.

Midwest City was a community with a high growth potential because of the war industries located there. William P. "Bill" Atkinson and his associates were building homes in the area, and they asked Goldman about the possibility of opening a Humpty store in the new township. At first Goldman was not enthusiastic. Later, however, he discovered that federal regulations governing the housing project specified that the development had to have a pharmacy and a grocery. After a series of discussions with Atkinson, Goldman agreed to lease a store building for ten years. He was to pay a fixed rent plus a percentage of all sales over a predetermined amount. The basic rent would be determined by the number of houses completed each month until a certain volume of sales was reached by Goldman's store. For example, if Atkinson and his associates were able to erect and have occupied one hundred homes in a thirty-day period, the rent on Goldman's store would be one hundred dollars that month. The building continued rapidly, and the grocery store was soon paying not only the rent but also a percentage on the excess volume, as agreed.

In addition, Goldman opened, renovated, and enlarged stores in Oklahoma City. One of these, built in 1942 on

Indiana Street, was the largest supermarket in the state at that time. The store was completely air-conditioned, featured fluorescent lighting, and contained its own bakery, making all kinds of pastries and breads. To keep pace with the many merchandise changes in the stores, Goldman leased a larger warehouse in 1941, and, soon afterward he leased two more to cope with the large volume of sales in the new stores.[1]

Flexibility and boldness continued to mark Goldman's business operations. In April, 1944, he leased a meat-packing plant in Marlow, Oklahoma, but the plant was destroyed by fire several months later. Undaunted, he acquired the Hill Packing Company the next year to supply his chains with meat. Purchasing the plants was the only way Goldman could obtain processed meats for his grocery stores. During the war years ration stamps were a continual problem for self-service stores. While clerks fumbled with the bits of paper, long lines of shoppers waited at checkstands. To speed up the process, Goldman devised small checkstands on wheels that could be hurried into place to relieve congestion at the fixed checkout points. Naturally, he turned this idea over to his Folding Carrier Company, which soon was offering SpeeDee Checkstands to its customers.[2] Another innovation he employed during the war was a series of cooking schools for housewives, to acquaint them with many of the new products stocked by supermarkets.[3]

Education and communication were always important in the Standard–Humpty Dumpty organization. Goldman insisted that all his executives attend the seminars and conventions which dealt with their own specialities. Staff meetings were equally important. Some unique developments in the operation of the business often came out of the staff

"That's my legal department!"

meetings. Virgil Sturkie recalls with amusement an incident that occurred at one of the weekly staff meetings at the Skirvin Hotel: "During World War II when meat was scarce and the government set the prices, we could sell whatever we could obtain. There seemed little reason for me to attend, but I still was expected to be there. One of the problems discussed was lack of soap, and, just to heckle the others, I suggested, 'why don't you just make some?'" The suggestion drew a laugh at the time, but the next Monday Goldman called Sturkie into his office and said he liked the idea of making soap. He added that, because the meat business was slow, Sturkie might accept the responsibility of setting up the program. Sturkie knew nothing about soap, but he learned quickly. Fred Young, a sheet-metal expert at the Folding Carrier Company, developed molds and a cutting board. All Sturkie needed was a soap formula, and he would be in business. His search led him to northern Oklahoma, where he found a woman with a suitable recipe for soap. The company started manufacturing soap in a former sausage factory that had closed for lack of meat. "It was plain, unlabeled, unwrapped lye soap," Sturkie recalled, "but soap was a rare commodity during this period." The stores sold all the soap Sturkie could make, which was a very large quantity, before the factory closed at the end of the war.

There were other wartime measures. During the war the government issued a regulation that bakers could not sell presliced bread, so Goldman devised his own slicers, which were sent to all his stores. One week after the slicers were delivered, the government rescinded the regulation. Not to waste his effort, Goldman used the blades of the slicers to make oleomargarine molds (oleo at that time was available only in one-pound bricks).

Courtesy Norman Rockwell

By 1946 the Standard and Humpty Dumpty chains were totally committed to the supermarket revolution. The next decade witnessed a continuation of this trend as Goldman increased the size of the stores and stocked a greater variety of food and nonfood items. When building restrictions were lifted in 1946, this process of reconditioning and building progressed rapidly. Nationwide, the retail food industry was moving in the same direction. Between 1946 and 1958 there was an increase of 213 percent in the number of supermarkets in the country. More than twenty thousand supermarkets were operating by 1958, and their rise in sales volume following the war totalled 637 percent. This growth in the supermarket industry reflected efforts by both independents and chains to increase the size of store units.[4]

Several factors explain the supermarket explosion, but basically there were changes in American society that favored the new method of retailing food. Beginning with the late war years, significant shifts occurred in the distribution of national income. Important to the growth of supermarkets were the relative gains made by lower- and middle-income workers. These increased funds soon were evident in food purchases. Not only did more Americans have more to spend, but also they tended to buy more expensive foods; the major increases were in fresh vegetables, fruit, meat, and dairy products.

Technological advances also helped alter American shopping habits. Automobiles, whose numbers mounted steadily in the postwar years, enabled customers to carry home larger purchases from supermarkets that generally were situated in areas with little or no public transportation. Goldman's grocery cart also helped bring about larger but less-frequent purchases. Refrigeration in both homes and stores added to the reduction in the number of shopping

"That's the super-market manager and his new baby!"

Courtesy News Syndicate Company, Inc.

excursions. Meat could be stored longer, and packaged frozen foods became possible because of improvements in home refrigerators and freezers. Also, the 23.4 percent increase in population recorded between 1930 and 1958 meant that there were more food buyers. More important, however, was the shift of middle- and upper-income families to the suburbs. A general decentralization of retail trade followed, in which supermarkets benefited enormously by locating in shopping centers.[5]

While these factors partly account for the dramatic rise of supermarkets in general, the success or failure of individual stores and chains ultimately rested on the policies and perspective of their managements. In this area Goldman's imaginative leadership consistently provided an impetus for growth. Realizing the need for competent subordinates, he initiated a policy of training and promotion that ensured a supply of responsible personnel. His success in this area became widely known. In 1949 the Industrial and Business Training Bureau of the University of Texas at Austin requested access to the Standard–Humpty Dumpty training files in establishing a retail grocers' training program.[6]

Goldman early had perceived the basic problem of supermarket operations—bigness. If stores were growing larger and chains were proliferating numerically and geographically, then an organization had to be developed to achieve maximum results with a minimum of effort. The job of top-level management was twofold: it had to set the goals of the enterprise, and it had to communicate them so that everyone in authority understood the company's objectives. For the most efficient operation, management had to mold the organization into a team effort, with all members fully aware of the chain of command and their chances of moving upward through the chain.[7]

After assuming full control of Standard–Humpty Dumpty in the early 1940's, when Morris Dreyfus retired, Goldman set about recruiting men who could make the decisions necessary in directing his organization's expanding activities. In 1948 he chose William A. Coleman as his executive vice-president. Coleman had joined the company two years earlier as general manager. Goldman searched for more than twelve months before deciding that Coleman was his man. Coleman's background included twenty-one years with A&P Food Stores. Goldman was impressed with the breadth as well as the length of his experience; Coleman had worked in store management, warehousing, accounting, and personnel. The wisdom of Goldman's judgment could be seen in the contributions that Coleman made to Standard–Humpty Dumpty, the most notable being the installation of the retail-balance form of store inventories, a system that increased control over gross profits while decreasing operating losses.[8]

Until the hiring of Coleman, Standard–Humpty Dumpty had always been a close-knit organization whose leadership had been drawn from the ranks. Coleman, who was from Indianapolis, was selected from a management position in a major outside company in order to provide the organization with his unique set of supermarket experiences. Coleman was the first and only outsider to come into the company in an executive position, and the decision to bring him in as manager came only after the entire management team had been consulted and each executive had admitted to a lack in the particular experience needed for this assignment. "I, as a Yankee, wasn't very warmly received, but they respected his [Goldman's] opinion in the matter, and learned to respect mine," Coleman says.

Coleman describes Goldman as a talented man, a genius with ideas and with the ability to develop the people to run his various enterprises. "He is always a hard worker himself and is able to get his people to work as hard as he does," Coleman says. "He exposes himself very little to his customers in the retail business, but leaves them to his managers and employees." In January, 1954, Coleman assumed the office of president of Standard–Humpty Dumpty. Taking over some of Coleman's duties after his promotion was a longtime employee, I. R. Moore. Moore had started in the retail food industry in 1934 as a stock clerk at a Humpty Dumpty store. He soon exhibited an aptitude for designing displays and organizing work that was rewarded by promotion to assistant store manager. Later he filled the post of store manager and advanced to superintendent of stores. He then rose through intermediate steps to become vice-president and director of sales in 1955.

At the time that Goldman purchased Humpty Dumpty, H. Virgil Sturkie was managing the meat department at the store at Northwest Fourth Street and Walker Avenue in Oklahoma City. Sturkie clearly remembers working an entire day and night taking inventory when the Goldmans purchased the chain. Although he does not remember his first meeting with Sylvan, he does recall a relationship that began very shortly after the store changed hands. He continued to manage the department for a time, and then was moved to the company's general office, where he supervised all meat operations. He recalls an incident that occurred when he ordered pork from the North at what he thought was an excellent price, but while the meat was in transit, the price dropped nearly three thousand dollars. "Mr. Goldman philosophized that you can't be right all of the time," Sturkie said. "His position would not have been as tolerant if I had wasted a half-dozen weiners in the sawdust." Sturkie notes that Goldman dictated his goals and wishes but did not dictate the methods to be employed in attaining them. "I bought meat for him for twenty years, and he never told me how much to pay or where to order it," he said. "I knew what was expected in profit and always tried to achieve it. If we fell short for a good reason, there was no problem."

When Moore transferred to Detroit, Sturkie became a vice-president in the company. Later, after the merger of Goldman's chain with other organizations into a larger corporate unit, Sturkie was chosen as the top executive of the Oklahoma division of the corporation.

These men—W. A. Coleman, I. R. Moore, and Virgil Sturkie—and their careers exemplify Goldman's policy about personnel and promotion. Each did an outstanding job for Standard–Humpty Dumpty in helping to build a superior organization. Goldman believed that advancements usually should go to men trained within the organization. His inclination to promote company men was based on something more substantial than sentiment. In 1948 he inaugurated a regular series of training programs covering every phase of supermarket activities, programs that eventually extended to all levels of employees and management. A special training school was established, and initial instruction and periodic refresher courses were mandatory. The curriculum was practical and serious, with courses continuing for several weeks; classes that lasted as long as four hours were conducted by full-time training supervisors or company executives. Employees attending the sessions received regular wages for their participation, which took place during working hours.[9]

Goldman showed his growing concern for the basic principles of human relations by starting a series of conferences in 1950 for supervisors and managers of stores and departments. Each participant in the conferences, which were limited to ten members for the five two-hour sessions, brought a personnel case history to discuss with the group. The problem would be analyzed and a proper solution agreed upon. Goldman believed that all employees in the entire chain would reflect the attitudes of management; therefore, it was worth any effort to help these executives and administrators improve their leadership qualities.[10]

A study of supermarket operations in 1961 suggested that few retail grocery stores accurately measured the performance of their employees. Fewer still, the researcher indicated, possessed any but the haziest notion of how to motivate personnel to excel at their jobs. Current management studies have emphasized the fundamental error of formulating policy in a vacuum—that is, ignoring the human element. A manager must communicate to his employees a sincere belief that the work they do is important and that he is interested in them as individuals. Workers should be informed about company policy and plans, and they should have a chance to express an opinion on them.[11]

Years before that study, Goldman was following all these rules in conducting the business affairs of Standard–Humpty Dumpty. Probably his chief organ of communication between executive and employee was a publication called *Super Marketer*. Goldman authorized its inception in 1947 as a mimeographed newspaper filled with notes about company personnel and short news items concerning the grocery business. Within two years the monthly publication was printed on rag paper and carried photographs. Contests, training classes, editorials, and informative articles on technical aspects of the industry stimulated interest in the company. In 1951 the newspaper informed its readers that questionnaires were being sent to each employee's home. Anonymous replies to queries about Standard–Humpty Dumpty management were requested. After the survey's findings were compiled, Goldman held meetings to discuss the problems shown in the replies and to suggest

The Neighbors   ▪ ▪ ▪ ▪ ▪   By Clark

"Well, so long, Evans. I'll see you again soon—at the hair-dresser's or some place."

remedies.[12] Through this practical concern for the employees of his organization, Goldman retained an efficient team spirit that contributed to Standard–Humpty Dumpty's tremendous growth during the postwar years.

By the mid-1950's the chain totaled thirty-three stores. None of the openings, which were attended by appropriate and well-publicized formalities, gave Goldman greater personal satisfaction than the inauguration of the store in Ardmore in 1956. He returned to his boyhood surroundings as an eminently successful businessman. The details of this store's opening also serve as an example of the art of "supermarketing."

Size alone rendered the new enterprise impressive. Eighteen thousand square feet provided ample room for the store's thirty-nine full-time and fifty-one part-time workers. The building was surrounded by lighted concrete parking space—enough for five hundred cars. The interior fulfilled the exterior's promise. Pastel shades of paint decorated the walls, and the floor, which would bear heavy traffic, was finished in rubber-tile. The aisles separating the shelves of food products were wide enough to accommodate three shopping carts at one time. Customers enjoyed air-conditioning, piped-in music, and fluorescent lighting. To facilitate speedy service, the store was equipped with the latest technological advances. The checking stands featured electronic counters operated mechanically by an electric eye that stopped each purchased item automatically before the checker rang it up on the cash register. A final belt carried the groceries to the sack boy, who placed the filled sacks in a tagged cart that he later unloaded into the customer's car after it was driven to the front of the store. Check-cashing services were handled at a special booth, which kept the checkout lines moving, while elec-

Just for Fun

Drawn for The Christian Science Monitor by Bill O'Malley

Courtesy Christian Science Monitor

tronic doors swung open automatically for customers leaving the store.

The new Humpty Dumpty unit's offerings of merchandise also reflected the latest innovations in supermarkets. The meat, produce, beverage, milk, and bread compartments were completely stocked from the rear. The proliferation of products also included nonfood items such as kitchen utensils and housewares. The store stocked an amazing variety of foodstuffs, including 48 counter feet of dietetic foods and 210 counter feet of candy, pastries, ice cream, pet foods, and frozen foods.[13]

Goldman's mother attended the opening in Ardmore as she had all the previous store inaugurations. She must have contemplated the vast differences between her son's ultramodern supermarket and the frontier grocery stores of her own earlier experience in Indian Territory. Gone were the bulk foods, crackers, and pickles by the barrel, along with sugar and flour in twenty-five-pound sacks. No longer were there the slabs of meat waiting for the butcher's knife to carve the customer's desired cuts, or the glassed-in counters containing a small assortment of foods which the grocery clerk removed on request. Gone also was the dimly lighted, fly-infested, poorly heated and cooled store interior. The contrast between old and new showed the great revolution in the retail food industry.

Yet there was a definite connection with the frontier past. In many ways the supermarket completed a circle in the history of the American consumer's buying habits. The center of retail business and social life in the eighteenth and nineteenth centuries was the village store or trading post. It drew people from wide areas and its presence in the community was looked on as a blessing. The trader or storekeeper never bothered with advertising; he was secure in the knowledge that his selection was the only one in

September 1942

The PROGRESSIVE GROCER

arthur crouch

Courtesy Progressive Grocer

"SIXTH COLUMN" at Work!

Courtesy Food Field Reporter

town. For rural Americans a trip to the general store was a festive occasion, combining easy one-stop shopping with the opportunity to meet neighbors and friends. The super-market's mixed lines of groceries and nonfood items, plus the flamboyant atmosphere created by advertising and store merchandising, reawakened a traditional American buying pattern.[14]

The initial advertisement for the opening of the store in Ardmore epitomized Goldman's merchandising genius. He purchased a full two-page section in the local newspaper to announce the supermarket's wares. Among the enticements listed were free gum, cotton candy, and balloons for children accompanied by their parents. And the parents could claim free cigars and cigarettes, coffee and doughnuts, orchid corsages, and plants. Circus rides were available with every purchase of $2.50, which could include specially priced women's hosiery, woolen comforters, electric frying pans, and chocolate-covered cherries. Nowhere in the advertisement was there a mention of groceries.[15] The opening was a huge success.

Goldman firmly grasped the ultimate goal of his stores: the selling of products to shoppers. Merchandising meant making certain that the goods were presented in an effective manner; in the supermarket era this has often been equated with sensational advertising. Mass displays have proved to be effective sales tools. Goldman employed the concept on a grand scale, sometimes with surprising results. One of the wartime shortages that troubled Oklahoma housewives was regular laundry soap. Near the end of the war, in 1945, Standard–Humpty Dumpty obtained a supply—first in Oklahoma in years—of a national brand of laundry soap. Goldman decided to offer it through a newspaper coupon advertisement. No one anticipated the fervor with which the women of Oklahoma City responded. In their passion to obtain the soap they bought every issue of the newspaper containing the coupon and then bombarded newsboys with demands for more copies. Later editions did not carry the special offer, and hundreds of women were

"MY DAD SAYS THE MOST EXPENSIVE THING ON FOUR WHEELS IS A SUPERMARKET CART."

Dennis the Menace. Courtesy Field Newspaper Syndicate

disappointed until the following day, when they were reassured that the supply of soap was not exhausted at all the chain's stores.[16]

On another occasion Goldman advertised a giant sale of breakfast cereal in a unique manner. To attract more than passing notice, a freight car filled with cereal was positioned on the parking lot in front of a Humpty Dumpty store. A similar idea was employed in 1955 to publicize the opening of a new chain unit in a shopping center: an oversized display—it was fifteen feet high—labeled "the world's largest shopping cart" appeared in the parking area. The huge replica, loaded with groceries, bore a prominent sign indicating its manufacturer: the Folding Carrier Company. There seemed to be no limit to the possibilities of selling by size. Once Goldman even commissioned a national dairy-products firm to process what was billed as the world's largest cheese—a circular specimen five feet high.[17]

Despite their magnitude, these merchandising devices could not compare with Humpty Dumpty's next promotional endeavor. On September 13, 1958, approximately 62,500 Oklahomans gathered in the University of Oklahoma's Owen Field in Norman to watch a professional football game. The event, publicized as the "Grocery Bowl," could be attended only by those who had accumulated the required totals in cash-register receipts from Goldman's chain. An unexpected repercussion occurred when a member of the Oklahoma House of Representatives, Tom Stevens of Shawnee, charged the Humpty Dumpty stores with unlawfully using state-owned facilities. When questioned about the accusation, Roscoe Cate, financial vice-president of the university, said that the decision to lease the stadium had been made by the school's regents. They

"The World's Largest Shopping Cart," a fifteen-foot-high model used in 1955 to publicize the opening of the Reding Shopping Center. It was shipped to many other states for use in store publicity projects. (Goldman Collection)

had accepted seven thousand dollars as a fee, of which one thousand dollars went into the stadium's operating fund. The remaining six thousand dollars was actually a gift that was to be used to purchase a high-speed computer for the University Foundation.[18] Representative Stevens said no more.

The postwar development of the Standard–Humpty Dumpty chain in Oklahoma reflected national supermarket trends in areas other than organization, operation, and management. In the early 1930's virtually all supermarkets were independents. However, the chains began adopting the new merchandising methods pioneered by their single, large-store competitors in the 1940's, while other chains, like Goldman's, were built from one unit. By 1950 approximately 37 percent of all supermarkets could be categorized as independent, single-unit operations, a statistic that dropped to 20.7 percent in 1958. Not only were the chains growing but also combinations of chains were forming that further consolidated the multiunit operations. This horizontal integration, or merging of stores and chains, was much more apparent than the process of vertical integration that was taking place at the same time. For example, vertical integration occurred when a supermarket chain owned a warehouse and provided its own produce needs or acquired a packing plant to process its own meat requirements. The obvious benefit of reduction of expense through horizontal and vertical combinations resulted from smoother coordination of the chain's various components.[19]

The Standard–Humpty Dumpty company achieved both vertical and horizontal integration. The Dutch Oven Bakery had supplied the stores with pastries and bread since 1932, while the Goldmans' past wholesaling experience had enabled the chain to provide its own produce. On January

13, 1951, Goldman purchased the Oklahoma Frozen Food Corporation, an acquisition that gave Standard–Humpty Dumpty entry into the fastest-growing segment of the prepared-food industry. Later that year he organized the Sylvan Drug Company to operate units in Standard–Humpty Dumpty stores.[20] By 1956, when Goldman decided to join in a merger of grocery chains, his own organization was already advantageously integrated.

Charles Allen, Jr., a fifty-three-year-old New York investment banker, engineered the merger that eventually brought Goldman into the eleventh-largest grocery chain in the country. Allen's conglomerate began when he acquired the ACF-Brill Company, a corporation founded in 1869 to manufacture horsecars. In June, 1951, Allen and his associates bought control of the concern. At that time the company was manufacturing 10 percent of the buses produced in the United States. Because this field was dominated by General Motors, Allen knew that his company's future was uncertain; therefore, he sold its manufacturing plant in March, 1954. The company then possessed cash assets of nearly seven million dollars but had no business or marketable product.

Two brothers, Nathan W. and John E. Lurie, approached Allen through an intermediary, Marx H. Hausman, with a proposition. They owned the Wrigley chain of sixty supermarkets that operated in Detroit and the surrounding territory in southern Michigan. Hausman, a semi-retired septuagenarian, had conceived the idea that he laid before Allen after having interested the Luries. The trio wanted Allen to erect a corporate structure that would hold together a group of grocery chains. The high-volume, low-profit-margin supermarket business would be amenable to such an increase in size. Allen's researchers revealed that

The Humpty Dumpty Grocery Warehouse and Office Building in Oklahoma City, built in 1954. (Goldman Collection)

during the first nine months of 1955 more than thirty-five mergers had been effected among supermarket chains. The financier also was attracted by the stability of the retail food industry and the high average sales amassed by the Luries' chain.[21]

Allen took the first step toward forming this corporation in July, 1955, when he purchased a 50 percent interest in Wrigley Stores. The next month the directors of ACF-Brill and Wrigley formally merged, becoming ACF-Wrigley and decided to acquire additional supermarket chains. On December 31, 1955, Standard–Humpty Dumpty's thirty-three stores and the Big Bear Markets of Michigan, which also controlled thirty-three stores, merged with the new corporation. Goldman simultaneously assumed the presidency of ACF-Wrigley and became a member of the company's board of directors. Nathan Lurie was chairman of the board, and John Lurie was executive vice-president. Norman Hirschfield, president since 1954 of S.N.G. Industries, Goldman's Oklahoma holding company, was elected financial vice-president.[22]

This new enterprise had a remarkable growth. Shortly after the merger the company purchased another chain, Foodtown Corporation of Cleveland, Ohio, and later acquired the Fred P. Rapp grocery chain of Saint Louis, Missouri. These additions raised the company's number of supermarkets to 148, with annual sales in excess of $300.2 million, making ACF-Wrigley the nation's tenth-largest food chain. The name was later changed to Allied Supermarkets, Inc. Goldman continued as president until January 28, 1958, when he was elected chairman of the board, and Hirschfield became president. Two long-time Goldman associates were advanced: William Coleman became executive vice-president in the Detroit headquarters, and I. R. Moore, vice-president of the Oklahoma division. The rise of these former Standard–Humpty Dumpty men was a tribute to Goldman's abilities as a developer of executive talent.[23] When Coleman reached retirement age, he retired. Moore was promoted to executive vice-president at the headquarters division and a few years later became president. Sturkie remained in charge of the Oklahoma division.

The corporation expanded in the years of Goldman's presidency and board chairmanship. Its phenomenal success was largely a result of the wealth of experience upon which the company could draw. The Luries and Goldman had been members of the Super Market Institute since that organization's inception, and the chains they acquired were operated by others with similarly wide but common backgrounds. Another acquisition was the eleven-store Bettendorf chain of Saint Louis. Further expansion came through enlarging existing member chains. ACF-Wrigley consciously tried to open markets in shopping centers that the board was convinced held the best prospects for high average sales.[24]

On December 31, 1959, Goldman sold his interests in the prosperous ACF-Wrigley concern and soon afterward retired from the grocery business. He was sixty-one years old and tired of the continual demands on his time and energies. His subsequent business career, however, would prove even more profitable than those exciting, competitive decades in the grocery and supermarket industry. He had played the role of innovator in every aspect of the retail trade, and would continue to use his merchandising techniques and knowledge of human behavior in his second career. Goldman's contribution to the supermarket industry stretched beyond the boundaries of Oklahoma. His membership in national organizations and his attention to local civic responsibilities had combined to add a not-inconsiderable dimension to his personal business career.

6. The Super Market Institute

The retail food industry was irrevocably altered by the advent of the supermarket. Goldman and others like him across the nation had worked independently in the late 1920's and early 1930's in developing stores and chains of markets. As the economy of the United States grew more complex, however, their efforts proved increasingly difficult. They were participants in a revolutionary period of the industry's history, but it was gradually becoming obvious to them that the marriage of technology and entrepreneurship, which had fostered the supermarket, needed some kind of central direction. Goldman was to play a dynamic role in the organization that would structure the new science of supermarketing in an orderly fashion.

By 1936 there were approximately twelve hundred supermarkets scattered across the country. Although all were components of a significant change in the food industry, none was very much aware of the others. Many of them had introduced new ideas concerning sales in their own stores without realizing that the same thing was occurring elsewhere. Ironically, the man who first recognized the need for an organization that could give cohesion to the industry was not directly engaged in the retail food business. M. M. Zimmerman, the chief founder of the Super Market Institute (SMI), was a writer who had ample opportunity to follow the developing trends in food distribution.

In 1914, while he was serving as a staff writer for *Printer's Ink*, he wrote a series of articles on chain stores. In 1931 his second series on the same subject was published as a book. The thrust of his study suggested that a voluntary association of independent stores constituted the best method of competing with the chains.[1]

Five years later Zimmerman wrote a third series of articles analyzing the techniques employed in supermarkets. His research for these articles convinced him that the new markets were a separate and unique phenomenon and that they deserved their own news organ, *Super Market Merchandising*, which he founded in November, 1936. With the aid of Zimmerman's trade magazine, supermarket operators began communicating with each other. After several months of exposure to their common problems and goals, they decided to meet on May 11, 1937, in the editor's office in New York. A twenty-three-man organizational committee was appointed to call a national convention of the Super Market Institute, to be held in September in New York City. The meeting would feature authorities speaking on mass-distribution trends, industry problems, and the organization of the proposed association.[2]

The charter of the institute specified that the organization not only would establish and maintain a cooperative relationship among owners and operators but also would serve as a central clearinghouse for research and data concerning the industry. When the convention was called to order in the Astor Hotel in New York on September 27, 1937, about a thousand persons were present. Most of them represented manufacturers and processors. Among the manufacturers who set up display booths was Goldman's Folding Basket Carrier Corporation. The invention that would contribute so much to grocery stores of the future, the shopping cart, attracted a great deal of attention from the convention members.[3] Only 124 supermarket operators attended the meeting; Goldman was among them. He listened to William H. Albers, president of Albers Super Markets of Cincinnati, Ohio, who delivered a speech emphasizing why supermarket owners should adopt a policy of promoting nationally advertised brands. Albers pointed out the need for grocers to build customer and manufacturer confidence by offering known brands at reasonable prices, something chain stores previously had not done. Albers emphasized the importance of demonstrating that the budding supermarket industry intended to be a responsible business.[4]

The convention agreed with him and showed its approval by electing him the first president of the institute. Zimmerman was named executive secretary, and Goldman was chosen one of the eight directors-at-large, who served along with six regional directors.

The next year the convention met in Chicago. Albers was reelected president, and Goldman once again was picked to fill a director's post. The attention of the meeting that year focused on the "Clinic of the Super Market," a program that became a mainstay of all future conventions. The clinic consisted of sessions on how to operate a supermarket. Most of the speakers, including Goldman, used slides to illustrate their talks. Goldman's presentation, "The Produce Department on a Self-Service Basis—Is It Practical and Profitable?" was later condensed and published as part of a series by the American Institute of Food Distribution of New York.[5]

During the war years Goldman never missed a convention. His wife accompanied him to the meeting in Cincinnati in 1939 and served on the entertainment committee.[6] Talk of war in Europe made the convention delegates uneasy. They recalled the accusations of profiteering hurled at some branches of the food industry during World War I, and they discussed the possible effects that the European conflict could have on the grocery market of the 1940's. They passed a resolution condemning profiteering and pledging to "do everything within our power . . . to bring foods to the ultimate consumer at the lowest cost." [7] Also on the agenda in 1939 was a panel discussion about supermarket trends for the coming year. Goldman predicted continued prosperity if the United States stayed out of the war. He also forecast the demise of the old-style supermarket, saying, "The day is past when a large, unattractive garage building can be used for a food market where customers can be drawn solely on price appeal." He did not discount the importance of low prices; he noted, however, that chain competition could meet the supermarkets' prices. Thus other features, such as ample parking facilities and attractively designed interiors, would be required to outdraw the multiunit operations. [8]

At the time the convention met in 1940, American involvement in the war seemed less likely. The bulk of the program that year was devoted to operational studies. Again Goldman was chosen to participate. His topic was "The Outlook for Super Market Expansion During the Coming Year." The general tenor of his and other speakers' remarks was optimistic. [9] Their optimism was soon to fade, however, as the United States was drawn closer and closer to the conflict.

The next four conventions were conducted in a war atmosphere. They were notable for the extent of government participation in the programs. The director of the Office of Price Administration and other federal officials and agencies briefed the delegates on food rationing and allocations.[10] In 1943, Goldman was asked to serve on the Oklahoma state committee of the Food Distribution Administration, and he added that duty to his lengthening list of wartime responsibilities.[11]

The next year some six hundred operators attended the SMI convention and they cast their votes for Goldman to fill one of the vice-presidential vacancies.[12] Goldman served in that capacity until 1950. The postwar conventions were jubilant affairs, with the number of delegates sharply increasing at each meeting. The organization had outgrown its temporary offices in the Super Market Publishing Company, and its size now warranted a full-time permanent staff with new accommodations in Chicago. The institute invited Don Parsons to become executive director, and he accepted in October, 1948. He brought a wealth of experience to the position. He had worked as promotion manager for *McCall's Magazine* and as vice-president of the Federal Advertising Agency, positions that made him extremely familiar with the national problems of merchandising. Within five years he headed a staff of twenty-five that carried on the necessary administrative work of the institute while engaging in their major tasks of carrying on research[13] and education and of providing a forum where supermarket operators could meet and exchange ideas. Parsons did an outstanding job in keeping the SMI well posted and was a great help to the officers during their time in office.

Goldman's reelection as vice-president in 1948 was a unique honor. Since he was already serving as vice-president of the National Association of Food Chains, his reelection to the SMI post made him the first person to serve in both capacities simultaneously.[14] The twelfth annual SMI convention proved to be most harrowing for

The seal of the Super Market Institute. The institute chose Goldman's grocery cart as its national emblem. (Goldman Collection)

Goldman, who served as general chairman. Goldman had been approached to accept the post, but for one of the few times in his long career he hesitated, thinking that an eighth-grade education did not qualify him for such an important position. "I was uneasy about speaking before a few thousand people," he later remarked. Moreover, he added, "I had never been an out-front man." The success of the meeting in Chicago led the delegates to pick him for the job of general chairman the following year.[15] Goldman must have wondered, half-seriously, if the institute's action in choosing its seal two years before had been part of a "softening up" process to obligate him to assume this task. The SMI device consisted of a circular illustration with the words "Super Market Institute—That there may be more for all" inscribed around it. The main figure in the illustration was his shopping cart loaded with groceries.[16]

So assume the task he did, and the 1951 SMI convention that he planned and led was another success for Goldman. In brief welcoming remarks as general chairman, the man who was uneasy about speaking before a few thousand people drew a sharp bead on the target—a record number in attendance. He also stated his concept of the SMI's function:

> This is a time to consider today, how to do today's job better, how to improve today's marketing so that its economy and efficiency will be a staunch bulwark against inflation which is the greatest single menace to our country's existence. We are first-line shock troops in the economic battle front. Though we are engaged in an intensely competitive business, we have learned to trust each other. We lay open, for all to see, specific, definite, practical ways we each have found to cut costs and to increase volume, that there may be more for all. SMI conventions are practical shoptalk among trusting friends.

If Goldman seriously harbored suspicions concerning his consecutive chairmanships, they were totally dissipated when, in 1951, the Standard–Humpty Dumpty chief executive, no longer reticent, became the fifth president of the institute, a position to which he was reelected a year later.[17]

In his presidential address to the Fifteenth Annual SMI convention in Cleveland, Ohio, in 1952, Goldman laid his personal business philosophy before his fellow members in these closing words:

> One of the marks of greatness in an operator is humility. This is an odd characteristic, I suppose, to look for in the busi-

nessman. But as I see it, humility is the gift of remembering that leadership is simply a greater opportunity of serving. It keeps you alert to see yourself as others see you. Humility is the gift that makes an operator run his business on the principle of "more for all." Because we have been given more, we must give more. Humility is the precious and priceless asset that makes possible an organization like Super Market Institute. It teaches a man that as he shares his knowledge, he decreases his own ignorance. And, finally, humility is the gift that enables a man to go down on his knees and thank his Creator for the great gift of being born in a nation like ours, where each and every one of us has the opportunity to serve. Let us go forward in service to the greatness that lies in serving America—in bringing to all the people the abundance the good Lord has showered upon our nation.

During his tenure Goldman had to contend with the problems of the Korean War and its effect on the entire food industry. The Asian struggle, however, did not divert the institute from inaugurating several new programs that greatly expanded its scope of operations. Finally, the Goldman presidency dealt with government officialdom in an effort to create a closer harmony between Washington and the food industry.

Almost ten years before the outbreak of the Korean War, President Franklin D. Roosevelt had established the Office of Price Administration and Civilian Supply (OPA). This agency, headed by Leon Henderson, was enjoined to guard against inflation brought about by World War II. By early 1942, Henderson's efforts to hold prices had become hopeless because he had no real authority. Congress responded to FDR's plea for legislation to correct this deficiency with the Emergency Price Control Act of 1942. Henderson, as price administrator, was empowered to fix prices and rents in special areas and to award subsidies to producers who would agree to stabilize their prices. The OPA issued a

General Maximum Price Regulation that was aimed at keeping prices at their March, 1942, level. But a large loophole in the freeze developed, and food prices rose 11 percent that year. Once again Roosevelt asked Congress for help and received it in the form of the Anti-Inflation Act of October 2, 1942. This law gave the president authority to stabilize wages and prices at a definite level. There was consternation in many quarters of the economy, but the inflationary spiral slowed to a 1.5 percent cost-of-living raise between the spring of 1943 and the end of the war in 1945.

After the war President Harry S Truman wanted to maintain the OPA. Congress contemplated ending the agency for several months before passing a weak price-control bill that the chief executive angrily vetoed. A few days later, on July 1, 1946, all price controls ceased, and the cost of living leaped ahead. A stop-gap law initiated months later also was allowed to expire, and inflation grew. Nevertheless, the economy exhibited a general prosperity until fall, 1949. Then in 1950, when fighting in Korea was suddenly escalated beyond a police action, Truman imposed wage and price controls. The Office of Price Stabilization (OPS) assumed virtually the same responsibilities as those of the defunct OPA.

SMI's membership was directly affected by every move the new agency proposed. An emergency meeting of the institute was called in August, 1950, to discuss the problems of doing business during wartime. The members realized the necessity for price stabilization to control inflation, and they passed resolutions favoring it. In December, 1950, the institute's board of directors hired special counsel David Ginsburg, Washington, D.C., to represent SMI interests that might be affected by any government action.

At the same time the board retained a Washington news reporting service to communicate all pertinent data to Chicago by teletype.[18]

The problem of whether to make a united stand regarding a price ceiling was acute. For example, the meat prices suggested by OPS did not allow a margin of profit for grocery stores in some areas of the country, while in others the level was so high that it was not attainable. In September, 1951, OPS regulations allowed retailers to charge $1.19 a pound for sirloin steak, but housewives in Oklahoma City probably would not have paid more than $0.98 a pound. From the government's viewpoint it seemed suspicious that SMI and other retail associations asked for widely varying price markups. Ginsburg reported to the SMI directors that their quick action in asking for a general price freeze in 1951, the year the OPS was created, had helped allay that agency's suspicions that supermarket operators were self-seeking.[19]

Price stabilizer Michael V. DiSalle had met with the SMI Defense Committee in February, 1951. The committee, headed by Goldman presented DiSalle with a special report outlining several steps that could relieve supermarket operators who were being squeezed by the freeze order issued on January 26, 1951. On behalf of the institute Goldman expressed the members' acceptance of these steps to halt inflationary pressures, but he also expressed their opposition to permanent regulations.[20]

Considerable friction developed between the OPS and the institute in the last half of 1951 and continued until late in 1952, when controls were loosened and finally dropped. Ginsburg experienced some success in convincing the OPS that up-to-date statistics should be used in setting price levels. Much of the supermarket operators' chagrin about

Sylvan Goldman (left) chairman of the Super Market Institute, and other institute members meet with Michael DiSalle (seated), head of the Office of Price Stabilization, 1951. (Goldman Collection)

OPS rulings came because price regulations were adjusted according to data gathered in 1944. Ginsburg kept reminding OPS officials that such rulings could be regarded as only temporary and that a new grocery margin survey should be made, subject to technical review by the institute and other retail business groups.[21] On leaving office in May, 1953, Goldman reflected on the complicated struggle to reach

156

workable agreements on price stabilization. He concluded that they had served the useful—but temporary—purpose of alleviating psychological fears of shortages. He was convinced, however, that such agreements were no longer needed, "and will not be again in the foreseeable future." [22]

At one point in the often heated SMI-OPS dialogue, the two entities, representing private enterprise and government, had reached an amiable accord. Goldman, while presiding over the institute convention in 1952, received a telegram from his Humpty Dumpty executive vice-president, William Coleman. On the morning of May 15, Goldman read the telegram to the assembled SMI delegates. Coleman's message urged the convention to act on the serious potato shortage, a situation brought about by black marketeers who had cornered the nation's supply. These profiteers were forcing grocers to pay extra for normal deliveries and were refusing to supply potatoes at all unless grocers agreed to purchase quantities of high-priced onions. As a result, food retailers were charging as much as $1.50 for a ten-pound sack of white potatoes, although the official OPS ceiling was only $0.80. [23]

The institute passed a condemnatory resolution less than an hour after hearing the telegram. The members were "of the opinion that the time for drastic measures to halt this despoiling of the public had arrived." The resolution also recommended that SMI members, together with all other food retailers, try to persuade the public to halt, or at least curtail, potato purchases and to substitute alternative foods such as rice and macaroni. This action, the institute believed, would end the profiteering and stabilize both the price and the distribution of available supplies until the temporary shortage of potatoes ended with the harvesting of a new crop. [24]

News of the passage of the resolution was carried on the national wire services. Ellis Arnall, the new director of OPS, commended the institute's action and urged American housewives to boycott potatoes. He denied rumors that his office intended to lift controls on potatoes, which he said were in short supply because of a reduction in planting the previous year.[25] The New York Office of Price Stabilization then assumed an active role in stopping the potato profiteers. Seventeen investigators, with headquarters at Utica, New York, were assigned to various parts of the state. Their probe uncovered complaints by retailers that they had been forced to buy poor-quality lettuce and other unwanted produce in order to secure the scarce potatoes. In Auburn, New York, restaurant owners admitted buying seed potatoes (such potatoes were not covered by federal price controls, but they were prohibited by state and national law for use other than planting).[26] Before the furor ended with the 1952 harvest, the SMI-inspired boycott had stirred a general debate on the federal farm program. Goldman and the other institute leaders could congratulate themselves on a highly successful publicity campaign that had enhanced the national image of the supermarket and performed a genuine public service.

The SMI also gathered statistics on profits in the industry. The costs of operating a store had continued to rise in 1950. Higher taxes and wages, along with the problems of price stabilization, were affecting the margins of profit in more than three-fourths of the companies that year. Only one-third of the SMI-member stores showed higher net profits, while the majority, 54 percent, suffered reductions, and 137 had the same profit ratio as in the preceding year. Because the food industry's profit margin consistently measured only about 1 percent of sales, these statistics seemed particularly ominous.[27]

Goldman once remarked that "making a living selling groceries was a tough, technical business." [28] This knowledge prompted much of his work as SMI president from 1951 to 1953. For several years before his election the SMI's board of directors had held midyear discussion meetings to complement the annual conventions. At the meeting in Hollywood, Florida, in December, 1951, Goldman presented two proposals. The first envisioned a continuing series of area meetings devoted to the practical aspects of supermarket operations. The second involved an expenditure of SMI funds for research activities to help increase productivity. [29] Goldman pointed out that the SMI had sufficient financial strength to support these programs. That factor, added to the apparent stability of the economy, created a favorable climate for the organization to embark on new programs. Goldman believed that it was time for a change in SMI policy away from day-to-day problem solving to a broader community-service philosophy.

Goldman noted that most SMI members could not afford to employ large numbers of specialists, or send representatives long distances to special instructional conferences. To fulfill the need for such consultative resources, Goldman suggested that a regular schedule of regional managers' meetings be inaugurated and sponsored by the institute twice a year, in the spring and fall. The nation would be divided into four regions—Pacific and Mountain, Central, Southern, and Eastern—for the two- or three-day programs. [30] The meetings would be devoted to specialized subjects, the first of which, Goldman suggested, could be fresh fruits and vegetables. Because the operating and merchandising problems of produce differed substantially from region to region, the programs and agenda would have to be tailored to each area. The responsibility for the meetings would be assumed by the regional directors, who would arrange for panels, speakers, and demonstrations. The cost of the project would not be high, because delegates would pay their own expenses.[31]

Goldman played a large part in developing the first round of regional meetings. He agreed to hold the first meeting in Oklahoma City. Four of the twelve program committeemen, including the chairman, were Standard–Humpty Dumpty executives. The program was totally practical. It covered the entire process of self-service produce merchandising from ordering to displaying fresh fruits and vegetables. The regional meetings became a standard part of programming.[32]

Goldman's second recommendation to the board of directors at the meeting in 1951 was aimed at research. Reports from many sections of the nation (in answer to an SMI questionnaire) indicated that growth was creating intense competition. Some companies said their only sales gains were coming through the addition of new units, while the volume of individual markets was stationary or dropping. The question of overexpansion was being openly discussed by some operators. Goldman proposed that the institute hire an outside firm of management consultants and engineers to study the problem of increasing production per man-hour in an effort to lessen the rise in the cost of doing business.

The study, as Goldman planned it, would go beyond a mere statistical approach. Professional engineers would be required to do field work at the store level. Their findings would not be limited to a list of minor techniques and devices. Instead, the end product of the study would be the development of a "labor expense control manual" for each of several kinds of organizations studied. Goldman estimated that the project would cost about fifty thousand dollars. He proposed an initial investment of ten thousand dollars to finance an exploratory study that would be assigned to an outside firm of management consultants. If the findings justified the expense, an additional sum would be appropriated to complete the study.

Goldman's research project met with virtually unqualified approval. The board actually exceeded his initial funding request, suggesting that the fifty-thousand-dollar figure should not become a limiting factor in view of the importance of the proposed study. Goldman had done his homework. He revealed to the board that he already had been in contact with two management-consultant companies—Booz, Allen and Hamilton, of Chicago, and Dunlap and Associates, of New York—that had submitted estimates on the cost of the study—approximately fifty thousand dollars. He realized, along with the board, that after the project was started additional money would probably be needed. The proposal was enthusiastically endorsed by a unanimous vote.[33]

Immediately after the meeting adjourned, Goldman asked William Applebaum, director of research for Stop & Shop, Inc., of Boston, to head the Research Advisory Committee. The choice was a logical one; Applebaum understood the use of methods and statistics as they applied to supermarkets, and he had made several outstanding contributions in this area.[34] Applebaum chose fifteen SMI members to serve on the committee, among them Goldman and Parsons, in an ex officio capacity. Later this body proved unwieldy, and the number was reduced to five. By the time Goldman left office in 1953, his original proposal had blossomed into a full-grown, ongoing program.

As part of this effort the SMI established a long-range research program to accomplish three goals: reduce waste

in food, material, and equipment; make work in the industry simpler, easier, and more productive; and improve the
techniques of merchandising, operating, and management.
To this end, liaisons with processors and manufacturers
were established. Applebaum expected the liaisons to produce cooperative ventures in research, attracting as much
as a million dollars a year. To handle the institute's part in
the joint endeavor, a permanent research staff, working
under Curt Kornblau, was added to the SMI organizational
chart. Under Kornblau's direction the first issues of the
Store Manager Guide were published by 1953. Every SMI
member received a free copy of this continuing series, plus
an extra copy for personnel and research directors. So
popular was this compendium of practical information that
each issue quickly sold more than two thousand copies
beyond the initial free subscription list. Within a short
period circulation exceeded ten thousand. Another product
of the research project was the "Figure Exchange." Compiled quarterly, this report analyzed vital operating and
merchandising statistics gathered from more than one
hundred participating companies in the first exchange.
When members saw the first report, participation grew to
two hundred participating companies.

Not all of Goldman's work during his tenure as SMI
president dealt directly with the organization and its inner
workings. As president of the institute he was called upon
to act as a spokesman for the supermarket industry. In this
capacity he wrote a guest editorial for *Food Field Reporter*,
a grocery trade newspaper. Goldman addressed himself to
one of the most pertinent problems facing all retail food
manufacturers: how to receive the fullest benefit from advertising dollars. He noted that grocery and food processors spent hundreds of millions of dollars each year adver-

tising their products and that this amount was charged against the cost of distribution. Such an expense, Goldman reasoned, could be justified only if it increased volume and reduced unit costs to the consumer through the economies of mass production and distribution. But many manufacturers were not getting full value for their advertising investment.

Before the advent of supermarkets and self-service merchandising, a strong and direct consumer demand was required to break the service-counter barrier. Open displays of merchandise had changed that system. As a result advertising now exercised a greater influence than it had previously (some products increased 40 percent in sales with the shift to self-service). Too many manufacturers, Goldman believed, had forgotten that this benefit did not come automatically. The supermarket still controlled preferred shelf position, special displays, and local advertising. These factors could affect sales dramatically. Operating on an average net profit of 1 to 1.5 percent after taxes, supermarket managers were inclined to use their merchandising skills to raise the number of sales on products whose manufacturers had adjusted their trade practices to meet modern retailing needs. Goldman therefore urged members of the food industry to make a strenuous effort toward better trade relations with retailers. Packages should be redesigned to allow for an adequate clear space, or "white spot" in the grocers' jargon, in which the price could be written or stamped. Shipping containers should be loaded so that price marking could be accomplished efficiently. Promotions and prices should be carefully planned to give the retail grocer a fair margin of profit. In summing up his argument, Goldman referred to the importance of the manufacturer-distributor discussion panels organized by the SMI. He suggested that manufacturers and distributors take part in the panel discussions and that they cooperate fully with the joint research projects sponsored by the supermarket organization.[35]

When Goldman stepped down from the presidency of SMI in 1953, he could view with great satisfaction the results of his and the institute's efforts. The regional programs and research projects were well launched and already bearing recognizable returns. The institute had waged a successful publicity campaign that had partly thwarted the machinations of the potato black marketeers. Membership in the institute had risen to 603 companies, representing more than 6,000 stores. SMI members and manufacturer representatives attending the annual convention in Cleveland totaled more than 12,000. When Goldman's term as president ended, an appreciative institute honored him with a plaque that read in part, "In recognition of his vision and leadership in guiding SMI into new fields of service through the establishment of regular managers' meetings and the implementing of a comprehensive program of research to further the development of low-cost mass merchandising."[36]

After 1953, Goldman continued to take an active part in SMI activities. He accepted no offices, but he retained a seat on the executive board by virtue of being a former president. Not all of his energies were devoted to the institute, however, for he also held membership in the National Association of Food Chains (NAFC) and attended the International Food Congress. The NAFC, organized in 1933, was composed of grocery chains, most of them also members of SMI. While SMI concentrated on research and education, NAFC was concerned primarily with government relations and public relations. Goldman, a member of

NAFC from its beginning, was elected vice-president of the organization in September, 1946, and served a two-year term. His duties were not nearly as strenuous as those of the same position in SMI.[37] Goldman contributed to many of the periodic panels and clinics conducted by NAFC. Although somewhat removed from actual store operations by 1958, he chaired the NAFC Management Clinic on Operating Efficiency and Productivity held that year. Two years earlier he had moderated a panel discussion for the national convention on architectural and operations analyses of new shopping centers and solo markets, a subject in which he was particularly well qualified.[38]

In June, 1953, Goldman attended the Second International Congress on Food Distribution. At this meeting, held in Ostend, Belgium, Goldman was elected vice-president and a member of the committee of honor. The convention featured discussions and lectures on cooperative efforts between producers and distributors of food, emphasizing self-service concepts.[39] Three years later a third congress was held in Rome, Italy. Goldman attended as an SMI representative. The SMI, along with manufacturers of food products, had contributed $200,000 in groceries, fixtures, and equipment to build an American-style supermarket in the special exposition hall on the outskirts of the city. It was probably the only supermarket in history with marble walls and floors. The United States government spent a quarter of a million lira on the exhibits building, which had been an athletic center erected by Mussolini. As flooring the supermarket had the same expensive Carrara marble that dominated the architecture of the remainder of the structure. More than 400,000 Italians visited the SMI and NAFC exhibit, which featured a completely stocked store. This display was set up to allow Europeans to see how food was sold at the retail stores in the United States, a lesson worth imitating in view of the lower cost of food in American stores compared to that in European groceries. The usual European stores were still divided according to the kind of merchandise—meats, produce, and so on—and were small, separate enterprises. The American model was designed to encourage larger-volume operations and free a greater percentage of Europeans' money for nonfood purchases.

At the end of the congress the American exhibitors offered to donate to the poor of Rome the $75,000 worth of food items on display. The SMI and NAFC exhibitors were informed that they would have to pay import duty on all the food if it was distributed. To avoid this payment, they gave the food to the National Welfare Agency of Italy, which distributed it to the underprivileged.

The Folding Carrier Company had sent basket carriers to the exhibit. When the time came to dismantle the displays, the Italian government advised Goldman that a special duty would have to be paid if the carts were left in Italy. Goldman responded by taking one of the carts to the American embassy, which was situated near the hotel where he was staying. He explained to officials there how similar carriers were being used by various government agencies in the United States. The embassy was delighted to accept the carts used at the exhibit, and apparently they proved helpful in handling mail and files in the offices there, because two years later Folding Carrier received an order for more of them.

Before returning home, Goldman, accompanied by his wife, toured several European nations, examining the state of the retail food industry in each. He discovered that Switzerland's storekeepers had adopted more of the modernized American concepts than had any other European country. England, France, Sweden, and West Germany were next in changing from the inefficient traditional merchandising of the past.[40] Because of overcrowding in most European cities, sites for markets of a size common in America were not available. Transportation also limited the development of supermarkets, because at that time few European families owned automobiles in which to carry home large purchases. The scarcity of merchandise, the lagging development of brand-name selling, and the inferior-but-expensive packaging also contributed to slowing the growth of the European food industry.[41]

Goldman's contributions to the development of the supermarket thus extended far beyond his inventions and commercial enterprises in Oklahoma. As a member of national and international organizations he did much to spread the innovative ideas that had revolutionized the nation's retail food industry.

The official unveiling of the bust of Will Rogers at the Will Rogers World Airport in Oklahoma City. 1952 (Goldman Collection)

7. A Businessman's Avocation—Philanthropy

By 1959, Sylvan Nathan Goldman had become a wealthy man and had retired from supermarket operations. In the year that he retired, he received a letter from Robert A. Magowan, chairman of the board and president of Safeway Stores, whose headquarters were in Oakland, California. The message was a congratulatory one marking Goldman's retirement. Magowan expressed his opinion that, while the Oklahoma Cityan "was not likely to find a hobby as engrossing as making money," he would "discover that it is almost as much fun to give it away." [1]

Actually, Goldman had started sharing his accumulated wealth much earlier. His philanthropies have been representative of his widely varied interests in religious causes, human relations, the family, the arts, and civic and national affairs. All of them bear the stamp of his concern for community welfare; several of his projects have benefited from his business acumen. The motives that prompt Goldman's generosity stem from his sympathy for the less fortunate. The broad nature of his benevolence and the length of his community service strongly indicate that his interest in the welfare of others has directed much of his nonbusiness activity.

Rarely has there lived a man of financial means who has not been constantly approached by someone with a proposition to help him spend his funds. Goldman has responded to many such proposals, but characteristically, he has also discovered little-known, but worthy, causes on which to bestow his time and money. Certainly one project was typical of Goldman in that he started with what seemed to be a relatively simple bequest and ended by setting a trend toward a vastly increased patronage of the arts in Oklahoma.

At a meeting of civic-minded members of the Oklahoma City Chamber of Commerce in 1950, Goldman listened as E. K. Gaylord, president of the Oklahoma Publishing Company, commented on the fact that the municipal airport, named for Will Rogers, did not have any likeness, such as a painting or sculpture, of the cowboy humorist. Gaylord's comment caught Goldman's particular interest. Goldman remembered that night in a theater in New York and what it had meant to him when, as a young soldier home from France, he had seen the Oklahoma cowboy star in the Ziegfeld Follies. This was his opportunity to do something in memory of Will Rogers. The next day Goldman was again reminded of Will Rogers. He received a magazine, sent by a friend in Texas, that contained a picture of a bust of Will Rogers sculptured by Mrs. Electra Waggoner Biggs; the bust had been given to a school. Goldman decided that it was time for him to move. He called Mrs. Biggs in Texas to ask if another casting could be made. She said yes and named the price. Goldman said that he would buy it. Mrs. Biggs then told him that Amon Carter, publisher of the *Fort Worth Star-Telegram*, had purchased the original and that his approval must be obtained before more castings could be sold. She said that she would ask Carter whereupon Goldman told her why he wanted the bust.

A few days later Goldman received a telephone call from

Amon Carter. The publisher told him that under no circumstances would he approve the Oklahoman's purchase of a casting. He would give a statue of the famous Oklahoman to the Oklahoma City airport. Goldman, his civic pride wounded, replied that his city was "not so hard up that it would accept a statue of Oklahoma's Will Rogers for its airport from a Texan." [2] Not content with offering to provide a statue for Will Rogers's home state, Amon Carter proceeded to nettle Goldman's civic feelings further by asking where Oklahoma's pride had been during all the years since the 1935 plane crash that took the lives of Rogers and Wiley Post. He claimed that his fellow Texans had contributed more to the Will Rogers Memorial in Claremore than either Oklahoma or California, where Rogers had lived many years.

This contention was later hotly denied by N. G. Henthorne, editor of the *Tulsa Daily World* and chairman of the Will Rogers Memorial Commission, who related the financial background of the Claremore shrine: Mrs. Will Rogers (Betty) had donated the land on which the memorial was situated, and state funds totalling $200,000 had been appropriated to erect the building. The memorial was dedicated on November 4, 1938. Five prominent Oklahomans had contributed the money to build the crypt and garden in which the Rogers family was buried. Carter had donated the equestrian statue which had been placed at the memorial's west entrance gate on November 4, 1940.

Only a few hours later Goldman received another telephone call, this time from Allen Street, the mayor of Oklahoma City. Street, who was at home recuperating from an illness, explained that Carter's lawyer was sitting in his living room offering to give the bust of Rogers to the airport. Aroused, Goldman quickly asked the mayor to reject the offer and to accept his own guarantee that he would provide a statue as good as or better than the one the Texan was offering. Street complied with this request, thus sparing his city the ignominy of accepting a bust from a Texan.[3]

Goldman had visited the memorial in Claremore, and he had been impressed by the magnificent sculpture of Will Rogers there, executed by Jo Davidson, the world-famous "biographer in bronze." It was one of two commissioned by the state of Oklahoma, which had paid $35,000 for both (the second is in Statuary Hall in the United States Capitol Building in Washington D.C.).

The sculptor had been shocked by Rogers' death in August, 1935. A long-time friend of the humorist, Davidson on several occasions had tried to persuade him to pose, only to have Rogers repeat a favorite sally: "You lay off of me, you old head-hunter." Wanting to keep Rogers' memory alive, Davidson asked Sidney Kent of Fox Films to lend him some of Rogers' movies to work from. Two cameramen installed a movie screen in the sculptor's Paris studio. For a week Davidson immersed himself in his subject and finished some small models that depicted the Oklahoma cowboy in a casual stance, "giving the world his drawled nuggets of wisdom and his precious humor."[4]

Soon afterward the Oklahoma legislature passed a bill authorizing funds to commission a statue of Will Rogers. Betty Rogers recommended Davidson for the contract. She sent the sculptor her husband's clothes; Davidson used them on a model to achieve Rogers' insouciant manner. Twenty thousand people crowded the rotunda of the Claremore memorial to witness the unveiling of the sculptor's art, an eight-foot statue that Davidson regarded as one of his best.[5]

Goldman, impressed by the sculptor's reputation, was

satisfied that Davidson's version of Rogers was the one he wanted. Goldman got in touch with the artist, who was living in New York, through the efforts of Walter M. Harrison, a close friend and a member of the Will Rogers Memorial Commission. The sculptor readily agreed to make a bust casting from the original mold, but there was a drawback: the mold had been stored in Davidson's studio in Paris since before World War II and throughout the German occupation. Davidson said he was returning to Paris soon and agreed to search for it. Some time later Harrison received a note from Davidson saying that the bust mold had not been destroyed. Weather and time had caused some damage, but the mold could be repaired. Goldman sent a message saying that Davidson should begin the restoration, make the casting, and send the bust to the United States. The bronze casting from the mold arrived in Oklahoma City in December, 1951.

On December 29, 1951, the Goldmans gave a party at their home, inviting their guests to "share a private showing of a bit of sculpture." [6] Later that day Davidson's bust of Will Rogers was presented to Oklahoma City, and on April 20, 1952, after a marble pedestal had been completed, the statue was formally dedicated. It stands today, as it did then, on a five-foot marble column facing the west entrance of the airport lobby. The Oklahoma City Chamber of Commerce voted a special resolution in appreciation of Goldman. Not only did the city own a work by one of the world's greatest contemporary sculptors but also Goldman's gift marked "a pioneer event in the beautification of Oklahoma City." [7] The resolution expressed the hope that the Rogers bust would be followed by similar gifts from other public-spirited citizens, a sentiment echoed by state newspaper editors. [8]

On January 3, 1952, just five days after Goldman gave the casting to the city, Joe Davidson died of a heart attack at the age of sixty-eight. The bust of Will Rogers was his last completed work. Goldman, who had not yet paid for the work, wrote the sculptor's widow to ask if she could use the money immediately while waiting for Davidson's estate to be settled. She replied affirmatively, thankful for the offer, and invited the Goldmans to visit her when next they were in Paris. Five years later, while they were vacationing in France, the Goldmans visited her at the studio, where she still lived. They noticed four pieces of sculpture in the artist's workshop and asked her about them. She said that they were extra castings Davidson had made of his favorite subjects and placed there "because he enjoyed working around people he admired." A fifth piece was on loan to a museum. At Mrs. Davidson's suggestion, when he returned home, Goldman wrote the trustees of the artist's estate to ask if the sculptures could be purchased. The trustees replied that they were available, and Goldman bought all five of them.

Mrs. Davidson wrote the Goldmans that she would accompany the pieces to the United States personally. She stayed as a guest in the Goldmans' home and attended the presentation of the pieces to the Oklahoma Art Center in Oklahoma City. Three of the works were heads: Abraham Lincoln in terra cotta, Woodrow Wilson in marble, and Franklin D. Roosevelt in bronze. The other two were head-and-shoulder bronze busts of John J. Pershing and Dwight D. Eisenhower; both were representations of the men as commanders-in-chief of the United States forces during World War I and World War II. All of the subjects, except Lincoln, of course, had sat for Davidson while he worked.[9]

Eighteen months later Goldman presented another bust

Goldman presents the bust of Will Rogers to the Tulsa Municipal Airport. Attending the dedication ceremonies were (from left) Richard Lloyd Jones, Jr., member of the park board; N. G. Henthorne, president of the park board and chairman of the Will Rogers Memorial Commission; Tulsa Mayor C. M. Warren; Goldman; Mort Harrison, chairman of the State Planning and Resources Board; Wade Whiteside and H. O. McClure, park board members; and Charles Short, Jr., airport manager. (*Tulsa Daily World*)

of Will Rogers, again to an airport. During a meeting in Tulsa, Goldman engaged in a conversation with the Tulsa airport manager and some trustees. They mentioned Goldman's gift to the Oklahoma City airport and observed that a similar gift would be greatly appreciated by the Tulsa facility, for Will Rogers had arrived there regularly on his way to visit his home in Oolagah (near Claremore). Goldman agreed to purchase another casting and present it to the airport.[10] When the bust was unveiled on July 27, 1954, the Tulsa Will Rogers High School band played at the ceremony.

After the presentation the principal of Will Rogers High School introduced himself and told Goldman about an unsuccessful effort by the alumni and students at his school to raise funds to purchase a portrait of Will Rogers. Goldman agreed to purchase the portrait for them; the money the school had collected was used to frame his gift.[11] The painting Goldman acquired was one of the only two portraits for which the humorist had sat. The artist of both was Count Analdo Tamburini, Italy's court painter. Will Rogers, Jr., who was present for the unveiling ceremony, expressed his satisfaction that the school was receiving the portrait. Rogers said that they were the two best portraits of his father.

Unfortunately, the artist's widow, the Countess Dolia C. Tamburini, filed suit in federal court in Tulsa to recover the painting presented to the city high school. She charged that Maurrie Morrison, of California, who had sold Goldman the portrait, was not authorized to sell it but only to exhibit it. The suit noted that the Goldman Foundation had purchased the painting and remained the owner, while the Tulsa board of education was named the beneficiary of a trust agreement that allowed Will Rogers High School to possess and exhibit the portrait. Countess Tamburini valued her deceased husband's work at fifteen thousand dollars and insisted that, according to the terms of his will of 1925, all his possessions in the United States had been bequeathed to her. The issue was settled out of court. In exchange for a financial consideration, the countess relinquished all her rights to the portrait, with a stipulation that a bronze plate identifying Tamburini as the artist be placed beside the picture.[12]

The construction of a new high school in Ardmore in 1960 prompted another Goldman gift, one that provided a tie with his distant past. The new school was to be named for Charles Evans, onetime superintendent of the Ardmore Schools. Evans had enjoyed a distinguished career. He had served as president of Central State University at Edmond, dean and director of the Department of Educational Extension at Oklahoma State University, president of the Oklahoma City Board of Education, and secretary of the Oklahoma Historical Society. Goldman obtained permission to give Evans' portrait to the Ardmore school, and he persuaded Evans to sit for the eminent artist Richard Goetz.

Goldman remembered Evans from his own school days in Ardmore and the two later had become friends in Oklahoma City. At the ceremony accompanying the presentation of the portrait, Evans thanked the merchant for the honor, saying, "nothing could ever have pleased me more." In his preliminary remarks Evans paid tribute to Goldman noting that Goldman had "come from severe and small beginnings and during his career has met fortune and misfortune and conquered both."

Concluding his address, Evans turned toward his friend and said with deep feeling:

It should be repeated over and over that there is enough of the God in every mind to grow it into infinite beauty and worth

Goldman with Will Rogers, Jr., unveiling the Tamburini portrait in the Will Rogers High School at Tulsa, 1954. (Goldman Collection)

Goldman unveils the portrait of Herbert Hoover at the Herbert
Hoover School in Oklahoma City, 1962, (Goldman Collection)

if but properly cultivated. Any mind is of God, and any of God
is infinite. The liberating principle of all life, which should be
the one supreme agent everywhere, is enthusiastic, righteous
doing; and its product, the supreme, climactic product of the
educational process, is "the enthusiastic, righteous doer." [13]

Goldman admits that the eighth-grade dropout of 1913 felt a
tightness in his throat as he listened to this accolade.

180

Two years later Goldman presented still another painting to an Oklahoma City school. The Herbert Hoover School, which adjoined a large Goldman subdivision, received a portrait of the former president at a special presentation. Goldman visited Hoover and obtained permission to have a portrait of him enlarged. When it was completed, Hoover signed it.[14]

Will Rogers was not the only famous Oklahoma son whose memory Goldman served by placing a sculpture in a public building. A private airport in Oklahoma City had been named for Rogers' close friend Wiley Post. Goldman contributed a bust of Post to be placed in the lobby of the airport. Not long afterward the city of Tulsa moved its bust of Will Rogers to the new airport it had just erected, leaving an empty pedestal at the old airport, which Goldman was asked to fill with a duplicate of the Wiley Post bust. Goldman commissioned Leonard McMurray, the sculptor of the bust, to make another casting. These were the first of several commissions McMurray completed for Goldman.[15]

A third famous Oklahoman likeness Goldman donated was Sequoyah, the Cherokee who devised his people's syllabary and written language. The Oklahoma legislature erected two new office buildings in Oklahoma City, one to be named for Will Rogers, the other for Sequoyah. Goldman was approached by state officials with a request that he give a bust for each. It was necessary to find Jo Davidson's administrator to make arrangements for buying another casting of the Will Rogers statue. The mold was still in Paris, and arrangements were made for the casting to be made there and shipped to Oklahoma City. The bust of Sequoyah proved more difficult to obtain. A portrait of the Cherokee was found in the Thomas Gilcrease Museum in Tulsa. Goldman, accompanied by Charles Nesbitt, then

The bust of Wiley Post was presented to the Wiley Post Airport in Oklahoma City by Sylvan Goldman. (Goldman Collection)

attorney general for Oklahoma, journeyed to Tulsa, viewed the painting, and arranged to have Leonard McMurray borrow it as a model for an original sculpture. Goldman repaid the museum by giving the institution a casting of McMurray's bust of Sequoyah. A few years later Goldman gave a casting of this bust, along with Carl Linx's *"Blackfoot Indian,"* an oil painting, to the National Cowboy Hall of Fame and Western Heritage Center in Oklahoma City.[16]

Several years after Mrs. Davidson's death, Goldman learned that the sculptor's sons were living in France. He obtained their address and wrote them about the possibility of obtaining another casting. The Cowboy Hall of Fame wanted a statue of Will Rogers, and Goldman intended to provide it. Negotiations were carried through successfully. The philanthropist was pleased to discover that, as it was with the airport presentations, no customs payment had to be made when this bust was brought into the country under the laws of the United States, the first six reproductions of any bronze are considered original).

Goldman's patronage of the arts was considerable, but of more significance was the manner in which his notable contribution was made. His search for the bust of Will Rogers demonstrated his interest in quality and his ability to recognize the right piece of art to fill the need. This ability was more than a manifestation of the competitive spirit that had characterized his business career. Amon Carter's offer had quickened his interest in the matter, but he possessed an excellent taste in art, as well as a regard for the sensibilities of artists.

In 1975, Leonard McMurray completed a nine-foot statue of Stanley Draper, a pioneer who helped build Oklahoma City and was one of the city's outstanding civic leaders. The work was commissioned by a group of interested citizens, including Goldman. Having dealt with Goldman before in similar contractual agreements, McMurray knew what to expect from his patron. Periodically Goldman visited McMurray's studio to check on the progress of the work. On one visit, not content with a cursory glance at the statue, Goldman climbed a ladder to study the sculptor's rendition of Draper's physiognomy, and he commented on several points having to do with the accuracy of the likeness. Far from becoming annoyed, the sculptor welcomed the interest shown by Goldman, whose suggestions, McMurray said, revealed a critical insight that he frequently took into account while working on the statue of Draper, as he had on earlier projects. McMurray many times has worked on commissions in which the patron virtually ignored the end result and never bothered with the intermediate stages of creation. He also knew that Goldman would take steps to have the artist present at the unveiling ceremonies and would include the artist's name on a plaque or some other device commemorating the occasion. McMurray recalls instances when such recognition was not accorded his efforts, but never when Goldman was involved.[17]

McMurray, whose reputation as a sculptor goes far beyond the borders of Oklahoma, credits Goldman with being a man of great vision in the artistic world: "He understands, perhaps as much as anyone in Oklahoma, the need for art work and for the development and beauty of the city, and he has the good taste to select and make possible items which will enhance the community.[18] Often McMurray calls on Goldman to evaluate a work, even those that Goldman has not commissioned, so that the sculptor can gain a fresh outlook on the project. For example, McMurray was working on a statue depicting Will Rogers on

Attorney General Charles Nesbitt (left) and Sylvan Goldman unveil the bust of Sequoyah, donated by Goldman, in the State Capitol Complex in Oklahoma City in 1962. Governor Henry Bellmon is at right. (Goldman Collection)

horseback. Morrison Tucker, who commissioned the work, was going to place the statue in front of the new Will Rogers Bank and Trust Company. McMurray asked Goldman to come to the studio, look at the work, and make suggestions. Goldman came several times to view the progress of the work. Once while he was there, McMurray told him that Dean Krakel, director of the Cowboy Hall of Fame, had been by to see the statue and had commented that he would like to have the work for his institution. When Goldman learned this, he visited Morrison Tucker to ask if he would permit two castings to be made of the statue, explaining why he wanted one. Tucker agreed to the second casting, and Goldman subsequently donated it to the Cowboy Hall of Fame, where it now is on display.[19] According to McMurray: "Mr. Goldman was so interested in this likeness of Will Rogers that he came out here many times. We went over it very carefully to get a likeness as nearly right as possible. Mr. Goldman comes with a fresh eye, and can see things that are really important which can be done to improve a work of art." McMurray describes Goldman's interest in the development of a statue as almost as intense as that of the sculptor himself.[20]

There is one bust in the lobby of the offices of Goldman Enterprises in the Citizens Tower that Sylvan did not commission—one of Goldman himself. The plaque on the bust reads: "Presented to S. N. Goldman in appreciation of his patronage of the fine arts, by Leonard McMurray, Sculptor." Goldman's patronage of the arts is characterized by his recognition of the need for beautification, his ability to distinguish excellence, his genuine interest in the progress and end product of the artist's work, and his careful attention to the ultimate setting for the art object. All these characteristics can be summarized in a single word: involvement. Many have given money, but few have shown the interest and expended the time that Goldman has. This circumstance has given his patronage of the arts a distinctive aspect.

The same qualities that have distinguished Goldman's patronage of the arts have also characterized his other philanthropies. His contributions in the field of human relations provide an outstanding example of his philanthropic style. In 1959, Donald Sullivan, the Oklahoma director of the National Conference of Christians and Jews (NCCJ), asked Glenn Snider, director of teacher education at the University of Oklahoma, to ask the university to sponsor a workshop on human relations for educators. Snider called an interdisciplinary faculty meeting to discuss the feasibility of offering such a program. After several meetings the committee agreed to establish courses for credit in the suggested field. The enthusiasm of the faculty members led the committee to propose a permanent center for the study of human relations as an integral part of the university system. George L. Cross, president of the university, responded favorably to the committee's proposal; he pointed, however, to the lack of funds for such a center and commented that it was unlikely that financing for the project would become available through normal university channels.[21]

The committee turned to representatives of the voluntary organizations that had called for the workshops in 1959 and 1960. Sterling Brown, a national director of the NCCJ, thereupon introduced the committee to Oklahoma City businessmen Harvey Everest and Charles Bennett. These two joined Snider, Donald E. Sullivan, and R. J. Clayton Feaver in creating an informal committee to expedite the establishment of a human relations center. Goldman was one of the first men asked to help with the project. At a meeting in Bennett's office Goldman stated the situation in his customary direct fashion: "Apparently what you need is $100,000 to guarantee operation of the center for five years." [22] To offset the disadvantage of approaching potential donors with such a high figure—and out of personal commitment to the concept—Goldman volunteered a contribution of $40,000 to underwrite the center's expenses for two years. During the next three years he reinforced his support of the center by vigorous fund-raising efforts that included trips with other members of the committee to Tulsa, Ardmore, and other state communities. He also attended regular meetings of the center's founders, constantly pressing for rapid implementation of the project's activities. [23]

The Southwest Center for Human Relations Studies was officially inaugurated on October 1, 1961, as a permanent program of the Oklahoma Center for Continuing Education. Its major goal was and is, "to reduce tension and conflict as it may exist between and among people or between and among groups." Included in this broad category of concern are race relations, religious group interaction, labor-management relations, school-community contacts, and problems arising from industrialization, urbanization, and feelings of alienation on the part of communities and individuals. To deal with these problems, the center offers workshops, seminars, adult education classes, and consultative services. It also engages in primary research.

The center's activities have been as varied as its goals. The Indian Education Unit has been energetic in its attempts to increase Oklahoma Indians' social and political awareness. Beginning with a series of organizational meetings in the western part of the state, the unit's staff developed the Southwestern Oklahoma League for Indian Development (SOLID). Concentrating on the Indian population of Comanche and Cotton counties, Lawton-based SOLID provided leadership in various services, notably a tutoring program in which older Indian youths helped younger children. It also conducted a continuing series of conferences on alcoholism among Indians. A subsidiary of the Indian Education Unit was responsible for publishing and distributing to Indians in western Oklahoma five thousand copies of a booklet entitled *Know Your Rights.*

Another human relations-oriented program was the establishment on July 1, 1968, of the Consultative Center for School Desegregation. Funded by the United States Office of Education to implement Title IV of the Civil Rights Act of 1964, the center sought to aid educational personnel in dealing with special problems occasioned by school desegregation and the integration process. It provided technical assistance and in-service programs to public school systems, held institutes for teachers, and conducted other activities that reached thousands of public school teachers and administrators.

Exemplifying the catholicity of the interests of the Human Relations Center was the Law Focused Curriculum Project, which was funded by the Oklahoma Crime Commission in February, 1973. This project was an effort to influence school-age students to think positively about the role of law in society. This goal was approached through workshops and seminars that prepare teachers, law officers, and legal personnel to use law-focused curricula in fourteen selected Oklahoma schools and communities.

The research and teaching functions of the center have continued to benefit from Goldman's philanthropy. In the summer of 1968, Goldman and Mrs. Leta M. Chapman, of

Goldman receives the Distinguished Service Citation from University of Oklahoma President Pete Kyle McCarter, 1971. The citation is the highest honor the university bestows. (Goldman Collection)

Tulsa, made a combined financial gift to advance the work of the center. The bequest was earmarked for the inauguration of the new University of Oklahoma Department of human relations. Goldman pledged additional annual contributions to support the S. N. Goldman Chair of Human Relations. This position would be the first of several which would comprise a department offering a master's degree. Within four years the new department had all the students it could accept in its master's program, which was one of only three such programs in the country.

Goldman's interest in the center has never flagged from his initial involvement in 1961. He regarded its work as essential to finding solutions to the seemingly insoluble social problems at local, state, and national levels. At a special meeting at the center in Norman in November, 1973, he addressed this topic on behalf of the center's Founders Council, whose members were honored at the event. Just as he followed the creation of works of art from inception to conclusion, so he regularly inquired about the progress and development of the Human Relations Center. Not only did he support it with his own contributions but his special talents as a fund-raiser were solicited by the center's administrators. The Human Relations Council was almost wholly dependent on such efforts during its first years and continued to be heavily supported by private donations.[24]

On May 16, 1971, the University of Oklahoma and the University of Oklahoma Association recognized Goldman's many contributions to the institution, the state, and the nation by conferring on him the institution's highest honor, the Distinguished Service Citation. The citation states:

> S. N. Goldman is testimony to the tradition of ingenuity and humanity. In his business activities, he has sought to meet the

Sterling Brown, of New York, president of the National Conference of Christians and Jews, presents a special citation to Goldman, 1963. (Goldman Collection)

needs of the public. Millions of shoppers and travelers benefit daily from his efforts through his invention of the shopping and luggage carts. He has been a builder of quality food stores, a developer, a friend of education, and perhaps most important, a champion of basic human rights and understanding.

192

Dolphus Whitten, President of Oklahoma City University, presents the Honorary Doctor of Law Degree to Sylvan N. Goldman, 1974. (Goldman Collection)

One of the many civic organizations claiming Goldman's attention was the Oklahoma City Chamber of Commerce, of which, as a result of his community services he was named a lifetime director. Stanley Draper, noted leader of the chamber, commented about Goldman's involvement:

His invention of the shopping cart was evidence of his creative genius, and suddenly Oklahoma City had a nationally recognized industrialist among its leadership group. Particularly after the World War II years Syl gave of his abilities selflessly to the major civic development projects in Oklahoma City. Regardless of what I asked him to do, and I asked for

Goldman adjusts the Eleanor Roosevelt Humanities Award medallion presented to him by Wisconsin Senator William Proxmire in 1965. (Goldman Collection)

plenty, he was always ready and willing. No project startled him. He promptly understood and added his great talent and leadership to make things happen. In all of my years in Oklahoma City few men gave me more support and creative effort than Syl Goldman. I really like the way he operates.

Not only did Draper have great admiration for Goldman but the latter has an equally high respect for Draper. In referring to Draper, Goldman said:

Stanley did an outstanding job for the Chamber of Commerce and Oklahoma City. He was not only a man who had great dreams but one who had the energy and determination to make them come true. He possessed a rare knack of being able to get the people around him to give him the support he needed. He was a man to whom it was difficult to say "no."

Oklahoma City was fortunate to have a man like Paul Strasbaugh ready to take over the leadership of the Chamber of Commerce when Stanley retired. Our continued growth and progress at an accelerated rate is testimony to Paul's dedicated effectiveness.

Goldman also was a founder, in 1955, and a trustee of the Frontiers of Science Foundation of Oklahoma, widely heralded as the outstanding citizen-sponsored organization devoted to improving education at all levels in the United States. In April, 1973, he and other founders were honored by President Richard M. Nixon, who invited them to Washington, D.C., to be recognized. Goldman also serves as a member of the Oklahoma City Mercy Hospital Advisory Council and the University of Oklahoma Foundation, and he is a research fellow of the Southwestern Legal Foundation. He is a trustee of the Thomas Gilcrease Museum Association and the Oklahoma Zoological Society, and a vice-president and trustee and director of the Oklahoma City Community Foundation. He also is a director of the Boy Scouts of America, the Young Men's Christian Association, the Allied Arts Foundation, the United Appeal, the Defense Orientation Civilian Association of Washington, D.C., and the Oklahoma Heritage Association. He has served as president of the Oklahoma Art Center and Temple B'nai Israel. Goldman is vice-president and member of the board of trustees of the Dean A. McGee Eye Institute.

For his service to humanity Goldman has received the Brotherhood Citation of the National Conference of Christians and Jews.[25] In 1974, Oklahoma City University honored him with an honorary doctorate of law degree and appointed him an honorary life trustee of the university—a

A copy of the November, 1971, document certifying Goldman's induction into the Oklahoma Hall of Fame. (Goldman Collection)

Goldman is "adopted" into the Pawnee Indian tribe and made an honorary chief, June, 1950. The name bestowed upon him was Nuchape, meaning "good, kind-hearted man." (Goldman Collection)

high accomplishment for a man without a high school education. In 1971 he received the Eleanor Roosevelt Humanities Award National Citation. Senator William Proxmire of Wisconsin presented the citation, which had been given only once before (in 1965 to comedian Bob Hope). On November 16, 1971, Goldman received official historical recognition. On that day he was inducted into the Oklahoma Hall of Fame, an honor reserved for citizens of the state who have made unique contributions in one field or another. Goldman was an obvious choice, for in his life he has made the state a better place for all Oklahomans through his business, civic, and philanthropic activities.

When Goldman was inducted into the Oklahoma Hall of Fame, the list of his accomplishments, read to a distinguished audience, was long—but incomplete. Many of his gifts and philanthropies, both in Oklahoma and outside the state, have gone unreported for many were given anonymously. His goal was never the many awards, citations, and congratulations that came his way; they were unsolicited testimonials to a man who had worked hard, who realized his dreams, and who then tried to make the world better for his fellow man. "If I had been permitted only a single sentence to epitomize my friend Sylvan N. Goldman," his inductor and close friend Jack Durland, said at the Hall of Fame ceremony, "I believe these words would best say it all: He is truly a mirrored reflection of devotion, respect and love for his native state, and a lifetime of dedicated service to it." [26]

8. Family Man, Humanitarian

Despite the fact that Goldman was struggling to build a grocery chain during the period that his two sons were growing up, family life was important to him. "Dad always took a deep personal interest in us, regardless of how busy he was," recalls Monte Goldman, who, with his brother, Alfred, is now involved in the Hawaiian investments of Goldman Enterprises, as well as other interests. "He was strict, but fair, praising us for our accomplishments, but never hesitating to sit hard on us for shortcomings," he said. "He was a self-disciplined man, and he believed in helping us to develop our own self-discipline."

Monte recalled a New Year's Eve party during his senior year in high school. "My parents were leaving town on New Year's Eve to visit relatives in Tulsa, and Dad instructed me not to use the house for a party while they were out of town." But Monte had other ideas. There could be no harm in having a New Year's Eve party for his friends, he reasoned. During the party the young people tracked mud into the house. Confronted by the evidence on the floor and rugs, Monte confessed, and as punishment he was restricted to the house for two months.

When the boys were in school, their father usually was working at his business. Breakfast and dinner often were the only times for the family to relax together. Summer vacations were annual family affairs, however, and the

Goldman with his mother, Hortense (left), wife, Margaret, and sons, Alfred and Monte (right), on the family's first trip to Hawaii. The child in the picture was the daughter of one of the dancers in the background. (Goldman Collection)

boys, and their mother and father enjoyed traveling and sightseeing together.

Early in life the Goldman boys learned about business from their father. Many times they would tour the grocery stores together. Alfred recalls that his father

> would point out to us things which were going wrong, just as he would the things which were going right. He would show us property which he had purchased and would tell us why he bought it and what future he expected from the land. Life with Father was a continual educational process. Dad would discuss business with us, even when we were very young. He would try to put everything into words we could understand.

Work in the grocery stores also started early for the younger Goldmans. They were on the job in Humpty Dumpty stores seven summers in a row. They earned the salary usually paid for the job they were performing. "My father had already ingrained into us that if we were going to do a job we were to do it right," Monte declared, "and thus we had no trouble adjusting to supermarket work. Since he owned the stores, we felt we had a strong personal responsibility." Sometimes this responsibility went so far as to bring the boys into other conflicts. "I remember having an argument with my mother," said Monte, "because she wanted me to take off from work to get some medical shots, and I didn't want any special attention. However, Mother did most of our rearing while we were young, so she got her way."

Monte's most memorable experience in the store was his first time at the meat market. After his first week working in this department, every finger was bandaged except one thumb. His original involvement in a business operated by his father, however, began long before he went to work in a grocery store. In a picture that appeared with an article in

Monte Goldman is the child in the basket in this picture that accompanied an article published by the *Saturday Evening Post*.

the *Saturday Evening Post* shortly after the invention of the folding basket carrier, he was the child sitting in the carrier. After the boys were graduated from high school, Monte attended the University of Oklahoma and Alfred the Wharton School of Finance at the University of Pennsylvania. Monte and Alfred Goldman are chief executive officers actively involved in the over-all supervision and operation of the many varied investments of Goldman Enterprises, frequently flying from their homes in Hawaii to the sites of various Goldman investments to contribute recommendations and expertise to the operation.

Mrs. Hortense Goldman, Sylvan's mother, was a favorite person to Humpty Dumpty managers and employees, who called her Mother Goldman. William Coleman described Sylvan's attention to his mother throughout her life as remarkable. "He took great care of her," Coleman said, "and called on her practically every day of her life during her latter years."

When his father died in 1945, Goldman was not content for his mother to live alone in the modest duplex on Northwest Twentieth street. He knew that too many things could happen to an elderly widow and that she should not assume the responsibility of keeping up a house and yard. Although Goldman knew that she would not agree with him, he quietly leased, redecorated and refurnished a lovely apartment for her in the Skirvin Tower Hotel in downtown Oklahoma City, at that time the city's most exclusive address. There she would have constant security, and help would be available instantly if she needed it.

While she was away from the city for a few days, Sylvan moved her into the new home she soon would agree was perfect for her. Sylvan furnished her a chauffeur and a new car so she could visit friends, but she would always visit a

Sylvan N. Goldman's mother, Hortense Goldman. The portrait occupies a prominent space in Goldman's home. (Goldman Collection)

few of her son's stores on weekends. If she found anything that displeased her, she would phone him later to tell him about it; she would never, however, tell a store manager or an employee.

Virgil Sturkie remembers one particular incident when Mother Goldman was visiting a store. She had a keen eye and noticed that the produce man had mixed higher-priced grapefruit with the cheaper fruit, offering all of them for the lower price. She stopped and bought a large sack of grapefruit rather than pass up such a bargain. At another store she noticed a discrepancy. At a third store she found Sylvan and some supervisors conducting a regular store checkup. She asked her son if he had noticed discrepancies at the last two stores she had visited. When Sylvan admitted that he had not, she asked, "Just what do you see when you visit these stores?" Sylvan managed to answer, "Mother, I was just waiting to see if you would catch these errors when you came along." Mother Goldman died on July 3, 1960.

Goldman's closest associates have described him first as a lover of people, a man who has a particular loyalty for those who work with him or who have performed well for him in the past. Sturkie recalls:

> We once had a young supervisor who developed a serious illness. Mr. Goldman sent him to the Mayo Clinic in Rochester for what obviously was to be an expensive operation. He told the supervisor simply to write a check for the bill when he was dismissed, and the supervisor protested that he didn't have that amount of money. Goldman answered that the money would be in the bank, to go ahead and write the check.

The man lived another ten years and then died, leaving a widow and two daughters. Shortly after his death Sylvan came into a meeting of department heads, asking which man would like to have the widow for his secretary. He explained that she did not have secretarial experience but that he would provide training for her. Today that woman still works for the Humpty Dumpty organization. When her daughters were married, Goldman was on hand to give them away.

"This generosity doesn't apply just to those who are working for him," Sturkie said. "A few years ago a Tulsa man who had not worked for Humpty Dumpty for more than fifteen years developed an illness, and Goldman paid his bills." Sturkie recalls many situations in which Goldman helped young men through college; in most instances, however, only those involved knew about it, he said.

Recently Goldman stepped into an elevator in a downtown office building and was greeted by name by a man in professional dress.

"Don't I know you?" asked Goldman, looking closely at the young man.

"I used to work for you when I was going to college," the young man stated. "That job made it possible for me to finish."

"What department did you work in?" Goldman asked, after learning which store had employed him.

"The meat department," was the reply.

"And what do you do now?"

"I'm a surgeon," the young man said, as he got off the elevator.

Goldman loves to tell this story for its humor, but a careful listener can detect the pride he takes in having provided jobs for several generations of college students in his stores. Moreover, Goldman notes that all his senior executives except one rose through the ranks of his company, another source of pride to him. His pride in others is balanced by personal modesty about his own achievements and contributions over the years.[1]

9. *"Retirement"*

In 1959, Sylvan N. Goldman retired from the chairmanship of ACF-Wrigley, which later changed its name to Allied Supermarkets. Thus ended his career in the grocery business, one that spanned four decades. Moreover, he had sold the ownership of Folding Carrier Company. He had sufficient wealth never to have to work again, and at age sixty-one he could have slowed the busy tempo of his life to enjoy travel, relaxation, and rest. Many of his associates thought that would be the case. One of them remarked to him on the occasion of the conferring of his second honorary doctorate that newspaper stories outlining his achievements "make you sound as if you died twenty years ago."[1]

Such stories were more than premature, however, for soon Goldman was more deeply involved in business ventures than ever before in his career. One of his first moves was to hire an assistant to help him with his business investments. The man chosen for this position was H. Arthur Littell. A Texan who had received his B.A. and M.A. degrees at the University of Texas in the fields of finance and investments, Littell was involved in insurance, investments, and real estate. Arriving in Oklahoma at the age of thirty-nine, he had twelve years' experience in his field, a background that would serve him well as he worked with Goldman; yet he would learn much more from his employer than his education and his previous experience had taught him. He later declared:

Syl's philosophy is that it doesn't make any difference whether you are selling clothes, real estate, savings, banking facilities, or groceries. Whatever it is, the elements of merchandising are the same. Syl thinks in terms of the success of each individual project or venture. A lot of people wonder how he can do so many things and do them so well. He thinks in segments. He knows that if each segment and each individual project or venture is successful, the total operation also will be successful. The only reason he can keep from going crazy with all of these different projects is because he thinks about only one at a time. If he solves one problem, he can forget it and go on to the next one.

Beyond this knowledge and this philosophy was an amazing amount of hard work. Littell explained:

In the twelve years I have been with him, he has never missed a day at the office, unless he was out of town on business or vacation. To my knowledge, that includes Saturdays and some Sundays. Syl Goldman's hobby is his business. Most people I know, including business executives, probably don't work more than 70 to 80 percent of capacity. Syl Goldman works 100 percent of his capacity. This extra 25 percent is often the difference between success and failure. Syl performs because he enjoys a challenge. He doesn't need the money for himself or his family. He works because of the challenge.

In addition, Littell observed, Goldman was a man of confidence. Long before a prominent clergyman wrote a book about the power of positive thinking, Goldman had come to understand this philosophy. Littell noted:

He exudes self-confidence, and, in turn, this confidence rubs off on his associates. He has belief in other people. He doesn't always make the right decision at the time it's made, but he can make a wrong decision right by his actions after making that decision. One of the outstanding characteristics of Syl Goldman is his tremendous self-discipline in his personal life, as well as in his business life. He's always the same.

H. Arthur Littell (right), president of Goldman Enterprises, and Peter Boatright, vice-president and treasurer. (Goldman Collection)

Littell came to work for Goldman in 1962. At that time Goldman was as yet uncertain about his future course of action. He knew only that he was not the kind of man who could remain idle. After several months of vacation he was ready to enter some new venture. His liquid assets, totaling a sizable sum, were waiting to be used in some way. Littell's job was to work with him in any venture in which

Goldman might become interested. This collaboration has been so successful that in fifteen years Goldman Enterprises has earned a greater amount than Goldman made in all his years in the grocery business. Of course, the Goldman brothers had started with practically nothing in a highly competitive industry. They had had only their own earnings with which to operate. Goldman's ventures of the 1960's and 1970's were financed with ample funds from within his own organization, enabling him to be exceptionally venturesome, but only with the aid of an extremely capable organization. He made fantastic progress in a relatively short period of time, and, almost unbelievably, every venture he has entered to date has been successful.[2]

Probably one of the reasons newspaper accounts of his life have ignored the growth of his financial interests since 1959 has been Goldman himself. On one occasion, when asked what his most absorbing business venture had been, he replied, "The only thing I ever knew was groceries— groceries and produce."[3] This statement did not reveal the many facets of his personality or his other abilities. For some years before his retirement from ACF-Wrigley, he had engaged in business enterprises that were not related to the supermarket industry. On July 6, 1955, for example, Goldman had signed the charter which brought into being the Western Security Life Insurance Company. This venture was the farthest removed from the supermarket business of any in which Goldman had previously engaged.[4] Nevertheless, the insurance company enjoyed a steady growth after its inception as an old-line legal-reserve company; in the vernacular of the insurance business, this meant that Western Life's premiums would be stable forever without special assessments. The charter had also provided that the company could issue health and accident policies.[5]

Goldman did not take a strong personal role in the Western Security Insurance Company as he did in his other investments. His older son, Monte, was active in this company and its organization. Monte quickly became a leading salesmen and rose rapidly to the rank of vice-president, supervising many of the agencies in other states and Puerto Rico. Goldman's younger son, Alfred, took charge of the real estate business and the Oklahoma holdings, doing well in selling, negotiating leases, and recommending acquisitions. Neither of the two sons, who entered the family business after university educations, seemed interested in continuing their father's supermarket-chain operations, despite their admiration for him. They had worked part time during the school year and full time in the summers at various stores, beginning as bag boys and later working in other areas of the grocery business including stocking and clerking. When they were in their early twenties, their father had acquainted them with his feelings about the grocery business: If Monte and Alfred wanted to be his partners, the chain would continue under their direction as they grew older. If not, then Goldman was going to sell or merge when the time was right for obtaining a good price. After thinking over the offer for a month, the boys told their father they preferred careers in some other kinds of business. Goldman later recalled that he accepted their decision with some sadness: "I felt as though I'd lost my baby," he said, referring to the food chain to which he had devoted so much time and effort. Still, Goldman admired his sons for their decision. He had witnessed more than one family situation in which sons had inherited a business in which they had no interest or aspirations, with resulting unhappiness and frustration.[6]

In September, 1966, Littell, who was vice-president in charge of loans and investments for the insurance firm,

Monte Goldman. (Goldman Collection)

Alfred D. Goldman. (Goldman Collection)

received a telephone call from the Gulf Insurance Company, of Dallas, Texas, wanting to know if Goldman would sell the Western Security Life Insurance Company. That company was interested in buying the firm for diversification (previously it had been in the fire and casualty insurance business). When Goldman was informed of the offer, he again called his sons into conference. He suggested that the two brothers consider the future by becoming partners in a single field—real estate—to guard against the eventuality of something happening to either of them, leaving the survivor entirely unacquainted with the other's business. Monte, who had spent much time learning the insurance business, agreed to switch his interest to real estate. He also agreed to the sale of Western Security Life. Accordingly, Littell informed Gulf that Goldman was interested in selling—at the right price.[7]

To ascertain the real worth of his insurance company, Goldman engaged an actuary firm to assess its value. The assessment report revealed that a large organization would pay less for Goldman's life insurance company than would a small one such as Gulf. The acquisition of Western Security Life would help Gulf diversify and make it a medium-sized company. In no hurry to sell, and possessing the actuarial report, Goldman gave a high "asking" figure to Gulf representatives, who, discouraged, broke off negotiations for several months. Eventually the Texans reconsidered and telephoned Littell at home on a Friday evening to see whether Goldman was still interested in selling. Through Littell, Goldman replied that he would sell for no less than the price he had asked initially and that no deal would be possible unless he was given an answer by early the following week because he was leaving on a trip to South America on Thursday. The Gulf board, anticipating a favorable response, had already met and voted to accept his proposal before actually hearing it from Littell. Thus the deal was completed within a few days; Goldman left on his trip only one day late. In the relatively short time that Western Life had been in business, it had been licensed in twenty-two states and Puerto Rico, and it had more than $161 million in life insurance in force with a premium income in 1965 of $2,653,157. Gulf bought all of Western Life's stock, which consisted of Goldman's thirty-five thousand shares outstanding; these were owned by him and his immediate family. The arrangement with Gulf left Western's management and offices in Oklahoma City virtually intact.[8]

The business in which Goldman Enterprises specialized in the 1960's and 1970's was real estate. Goldman's interest in this field stemmed directly from his earlier experiences in supermarketing. In fact, the two facets of his business career were natural partners. The years he had spent searching for available and suitable supermarket sites were good training for success in his new field. Because most of his new supermarkets were built in suburban areas, Goldman gradually moved more and more closely into that retail phenomenon of the post–World War II period, the shopping center. In time he acquired several properties that were beyond the fringe of what then was the populated area of Oklahoma City.

On April 20, 1955, Goldman Enterprises announced plans for a shopping center in southwest Oklahoma City as a result of a land purchase Goldman had made some time before. According to the newspaper account Goldman had paid more than he intended for the land on which the shopping center would be built. Nick N. Reding, the original owner, had been reluctant to sell the tract, which was

Part of the Reding Shopping Center, Oklahoma City, built by Goldman Enterprises. (Goldman Collection)

part of his farm. Eager to obtain the land because of what he saw as a future advantageous location, Goldman, after months of fruitless negotiations with Reding, raised his buying price and offered a method of payment that would give the seller a tax break. To convince Reding, Goldman painted a glowing verbal picture of the future large and attractive shopping center, which he said he would call Reding's, and he promised he would mount a large neon sign with Reding's name above it.[9]

By early September the shopping center was still six weeks from completion—bad weather in May had caused material damage to the construction site. Despite these delays the center finally opened formally on October 20. The edifice was strictly modern in appearance and construction. The main architectural feature of the complex, the largest in Oklahoma City up to that time, was an overwhelming expanse of plate glass relieved only by shop partitions, aluminum strips, and doors. A granite base with stone trim decorated the facade of the brick structure, which was completely air-conditioned. In keeping with the modernistic design, the center's largest store, a Humpty Dumpty market, contained the latest twist in supermarketing technology, a powered food conveyor. Loaded sacks of groceries could be placed on the conveyor belt and moved through openings in the plate-glass window to the sidewalk, where Humpty Dumpty employees would be waiting to load the bags into customers' cars.

The entire shopping-center sidewalk was equipped with a twelve-foot, aluminum-covered canopy, a feature that was included for two reasons: it afforded shoppers protection from bad weather and it eliminated storefront parking, thus avoiding traffic congestion. Another inducement for shopping several stores on foot was the provision of free strollers for carting children along the mall. All the "ballyhoo" associated with a supermarket opening attended the grand opening of the center. The city's largest shopping center also boasted what was advertised as the community's biggest neon sign. A free circus that could entertain two thousand persons at a time performed for two weeks.[10]

The Reding Shopping Center was a trend-continuing project that eventually was to alter the retail-merchandising pattern of Oklahoma City. Most of the tenants of the complex were branch operations of downtown establishments.[11] In 1955 this expansion of downtown stores into the suburbs was not regarded as an ominous sign of the future decay of the inner city, but subsequent events proved that it was. Goldman was one of the earliest to recognize the importance of Oklahoma City's tendency to sprawl in every direction from the downtown area. Without an effective commercial mass-transit system the suburban shopping center was the natural alternative to driving long distances to the downtown area, which increasingly was plagued with traffic congestion and expensive parking.

As the population moved out to areas surrounding his original land purchases, Goldman made additional acquisitions. In 1956 his Almonte Development Company, named for his sons, publicized plans for a residential subdivision to be situated southwest of Oklahoma City (west of May Avenue from Southwest Fifty-third to Southwest Fifty-ninth streets). When fully developed, this subdivision covered approximately 265 acres. A shopping center utilizing twenty-seven acres of the area served a large number of homes. The company exercised architectural supervision, installed the streets and water and sewer lines, and then sold the lots to home builders.

Goldman was thus no novice at real estate development in 1962, when Littell joined in helping reshape his financial investments. After they agreed on the kind and geography of the diversification, Goldman's holdings spread until the term "business empire" would not have been an exaggeration. When Goldman sold his grocery chain and the Folding Carrier Corporation, his extensive real estate holdings in Tulsa and Oklahoma City (acquired for development and expansion of his businesses) had not been included. In the years since Littell joined the firm, the basic pattern of Goldman Enterprises has remained fairly constant, with Goldman serving as chairman of the board, his two sons as cochairmen of the board, and Littell as president. Littell does an outstanding job of investigating and suggesting areas for investment, and Goldman adds his merchandising talents.

By 1976, Goldman's interests were scattered over several cities and states, including Hawaii and Puerto Rico. His two major concerns were real estate development and savings and loan institutions. Almost all of the ventures are fully owned businesses, while a few are joint projects with associate investors under the direction of Goldman Enterprises. Included in the planned diversification program are apartment complexes in Atlanta, Houston, and San Juan, Puerto Rico; housing and commercial developments in Houston, Dallas, and Tucson; and banking and savings and loan companies in Houston and several Colorado cities, including Denver. Not all these investments met with Goldman's initial approval, but all have proved successful.

To guard against failure, Goldman has always kept in mind the basic business principles that he evolved in building his grocery chain. All of his accumulated knowledge about merchandising and financial dealings can be reduced to a common denominator—understanding people. Just as a successful politician usually develops a feeling for how his constituents will react in a given situation, so a businessman learns to gauge in advance what will appeal to his customers. In most instances that involved the selling of an idea or product, Goldman applied the techniques he had learned while vending groceries.

The Otero Saving and Loan Association of La Junta, Colorado, a relatively small, one-location business, was one of those opportunities for investment that Goldman undertook reluctantly. He had had no experience with savings and loan institutions, but he was trying to help a friend who was interested in purchasing the association. Once embarked on that course, however, he felt no qualms. Goldman attempted to ensure the vindication of the investment at Otero by recalling a lesson he had learned in the past. When he had purchased grocery stores in Oklahoma

The Otero Savings and Loan Building, Colorado Spring, Colorado. (Goldman Collection)

City during the Depression years, he had not changed the names of the stores at first on the theory that people enjoy the sense of dealing with a known, local institution.[12] When Goldman Enterprises later accepted full control of the small Colorado savings and loan company, he made no sweeping changes in personnel. The company had been sold because its president, who had operated it during most of its existence, wanted to retire. Goldman persuaded Merle C. Carpenter, now president of the company and chairman of the board, to leave a savings and loan organization in Pueblo, Colorado, to take charge of the firm, encouraging him to retain the flavor of a home-owned and home-operated business while expanding the scope of the institution's activities. The firm's advertising notes that it was founded in Otero County, Colorado, "87 years ago in July, 1890." Reflecting the pride in a common heritage that all Coloradans in the area felt, the association adopted as its company emblem the six flags that had flown over the area—those of the United States, Colorado, Texas, Spain, France, and Mexico. Otero's publicity focuses less on the firm's considerable assets—in excess of $180 million— than on its link with local history.

When purchased, Otero had $5 million on deposit after operating from 1890 to the 1960's. A few years elapsed before the company was able to get permission to open a branch in Pueblo, then a branch in Colorado Springs and one in Denver. In 1974 another branch was added in Colorado Springs, another in Widefield, and another in Walsenburg. A second branch in Denver was completed in 1975. After eleven years under Goldman's control Otero deposits exceeded $120 million.[13] It is the tenth-largest savings and loan association in the state.

Far different from the Otero involvement was Goldman's venture in Puerto Rico. A friend had urged Goldman to join him in an investment on the island. Preoccupied with matters in Oklahoma, Goldman was not really interested, but he put up the money requested with the stipulation that his friend not bother him with the details of the business, a manufacturing concern that made kitchen cabinets. After a time Goldman and another partner in Colorado were asked to take a joint vacation to Puerto Rico. Goldman accepted the invitation but once again mentioned that he did not want to see the cabinet plant or discuss it. Inevitably, during the stay at San Juan the visitors found themselves making a

The ten-acre Santa Maria Shopping Center in San Juan, Puerto Rico, owned by Goldman Enterprises. (Goldman Collection)

tour of the countryside. A drizzling rain provided an excuse to stop at a building that just happened to house the factory.

While walking through the layout, Goldman learned that the operation was losing money because there was not a steady demand for the product. When the firm bid on a contract for kitchen cabinets and got the job, the workers were often busy day and night; at other times, when the company failed to secure contracts, the plant would all but shut down for lack of business. Yet the sizable cost of retaining key personnel and paying for normal expenses

continued. Despite his claim that he was not interested, Goldman could not help pointing out some improvements that could be made on the production line, which was not automated or efficient. He also suggested a solution to the merchandising problem. He proposed buying local real estate and developing it for builders. That would create a steady market for kitchen cabinets.

One of the partners knew of an available piece of land, and the group purchased it. Goldman had not wanted to get into home building, but the others, who were homebuilders, were in favor of such a move. Realizing that this development would increase the value of the adjacent land, Goldman urged the group to buy the adjoining real estate.

Architect's concept of the San José Office Building in San José, Puerto Rico, a Goldman Enterprises investment. (Goldman Collection)

His partners agreed, but the high asking price changed their minds. Goldman thereupon said that he would buy it himself and his partners could have thirty days in which to change their minds and join him in the deal. By the end of that period they had reconsidered and decided to join him.

From this somewhat reluctant beginning, Goldman's Puerto Rican investments grew to include not only land but also the first regional shopping center in Puerto Rico, a ten-story office building, three twelve-story apartment houses, and various other real estate projects. After several years the partners sold most of their holdings and dissolved the partnership. Goldman, however, has continued to expand on the island, and he now owns considerable properties in San Juan.[14] Peter Boatright, vice-president and treasurer of Goldman Enterprises, who has degrees in law and business from the University of Oklahoma, and also is a certified public accountant, was extremely helpful in the development of these interests, because the situation in Puerto Rico differs in many respects from the system on the mainland.

Boatright says that he has received more than a salary from his employer. He credits Goldman with getting him to stop smoking. Goldman, although not a health addict, pays close attention to his weight, exercises regularly, and does not smoke. As a result he maintains a healthy, trim appearance and a youthful vigor—and he recommends his regimen to his employees. When Boatright came to work for Goldman, Boatright had smoked for twenty years. Whenever Goldman found an article on the dangers of using tobacco, he would clip it and give it to Boatright. Once, after Goldman found a particularly shocking article about smoking, he said, "Pete, you are going to have to give up those cigarettes or you will kill yourself."

"The way he said it made me decide he was right," Boatright recalls. "At that moment I pulled a package of cigarettes from my pocket and threw it in the wastebasket." Today, nine years later, Boatright still does not smoke.

Boatright has observed some of the secrets of Goldman's success, especially his willingness to adapt:

> Syl Goldman is never afraid of new ideas. He might come into my office with a clipping from a newspaper about a new computer or other equipment and ask me to check it out to see if it applies to the business. If he ever hands you a clipping of this sort, there's nothing to do but to check it out, because Syl will not forget it. Before long he will be asking about it again.

One of Boatright's stories about his employer involves a particular painting that hangs in the office of Goldman Enterprises. This picture, by Leslie Ross, shows a cowboy and his girl hanging onto the reins of a runaway buckboard. Roscoe Fawcett, of Fawcett Publications, sent the picture to Goldman several years ago. Fawcett had called Sylvan to invite him along on a fishing trip to Canada. Goldman replied that he could not go because he was too busy with his supermarkets and the Folding Carrier Company. Fawcett and his guests went without Goldman, but upon his return Fawcett sent the painting to Sylvan. Attached to it was a note stating, "You just can't let go of the reins, can you?" [15]

Goldman's cautious approach to some of his investments was equally evident when he shared in a venture in Houston, Texas. Despite his investing a large amount of money in Regency Square, an office-retail-residential development, Goldman's name has not been prominent in the publicity surrounding the project. Instead, the firm of Marvin E. Leggett and Associates, Houston residential and commercial developers, and Anrem Corporation, a subsidiary

BORINQUEN TOWERS · RIO PIEDRAS · PUERTO RICO
V. MUÑIZ NUÑEZ · SARGENT · WEBSTER · CRENSHAW & FOLLEY · ASSOCIATED ARCH

One of Goldman's island enterprises is the Borinquen Towers in San Juan, Puerto Rico. (Goldman Collection)

of American National Insurance Company, were named as the developers. Leggett has been associated with other of Goldman's real estate projects in Houston since 1964, but few businessmen there are aware of the connection. Goldman believes that resentful developers might have placed obstacles in the project's path had it been known that a major Oklahoma developer was involved.

The Regency Square project, announced in September, 1971, began construction in 1972 of what its publicity releases termed "the Golden Micropolis." It encompasses

The Texas Bank and Trust Tower and Colonial Savings Tower, in
Regency Square in Houston, Texas. (Goldman Collection)

125 acres at the corner of Houston's Southwest Freeway and Hillcroft Drive, bounded on the north by Harwin Drive. The twelve-story Texas Bank and Trust Tower was the first of fourteen projected office buildings to be completed. The structure contains 234,000 square feet of floor space and has a garage for 893 cars. By 1977, 350 condominium apartments had been built, three other office buildings had been completed, and five more were under construction, including a duplicate of the Texas Bank and Trust Tower, which is now the home office of the Colonial Savings Association and named Colonial Savings Tower. On the board of directors of both Texas Bank and Trust and Colonial Savings Association are Goldman, Littell and Leggett. The decision to enter the banking business in Houston was made with the opening of Texas Bank and Trust in late 1972. Five and one-half years later total resources of the bank exceeded $32 million. In 1973, Goldman Enterprises added the Colonial Savings Association, with four branches and $25 million in assets, to its Houston investments. By mid-1978 Colonial had tripled in size to ten branches and more than $76 million in assets.

Other Goldman real estate projects in which Leggett has been associated include the 480-acre Lakeside Estates and Lakeside Forest, the 478-acre Green Ridge North, the 353-acre Prestonwood Forest, the 483-acre Willowood, the 859-acre Northwest Park, and the 2,600-acre Williamsburg on Houston's Katy Freeway.

Goldman's Houston associates include Donald McGregor, Sr., and Donald McGregor, Jr. Together they own the Ramada Inn Southwest, the 250-acre Inverness Forest residential development, and the 300-acre Lexington Woods project. When it was purchased in 1966, the motel had 125 rooms with a sizable area of land adjoining. It has been expanded to 315 rooms. In mid-1977 con-

"The Golden Micropolis," the Regency Square project.
(Goldman Collection)

struction began on the adjoining 8-story, 140-room Ramada
Tower, creating a total of 455 rooms, making it one of
Ramada's largest. During the past several years, Goldman
has also moved into another Texas city, Dallas, where

The Ramada Inn Southwest, Houston. (Goldman Collection)

George Poston, a Dallas realtor, has been his associate in acquiring substantial acreages. Their properties in the Dallas area include 1,084 acres on the west side of prestigious Preston Road, just north of FM 544; 170 acres on Preston Road at Frankfort Road, just north of Preston Trails Country Club; 160 acres adjoining Willow Bend Polo and Hunt Club; and 195 acres on Highway 289 in Plano, adjoining Hunter's Glen Subdivision.

Completed in Tucson, Arizona, are the 80-acre El Dorado Hills Subdivision, the Skyline Bel Air Plaza Shopping Center, the 600-acre Skyline Bel Air Estates, and the

The Skyline Bel Air Plaza Shopping Center in Tucson, Arizona. (Goldman Collection)

677-acre Bel Air Ranch Estates. Goldman retains ownership of Tanque Verde Water Company, which serves a large area adjoining Tucson on the east.

Obviously Goldman, at age seventy-eight, has not "retired" in the ordinary sense of the word. Most individuals at a similar stage in life would be reluctant, if indeed physically and mentally able, to continue to enter new fields of business endeavor. Yet Goldman has set an unusual standard of success in his years of retirement.

A man who has achieved almost eight decades of life and possesses great wealth and yet maintains a routine of work might be suspected of being driven by habit or compulsion. But Goldman's devotion to his business can be explained in other ways. He has felt no need to escape to the golf course for relaxation, because he does not suffer from tension or apprehension as the result of his daily attention to business detail. The intricacies of finance and merchandising offer a familiar and welcome challenge, free of attendant worries. For Goldman his vocation has also been—and is—an enjoyable avocation.

Some social scientists and social critics have condemned American businessmen for devoting their careers to making money. The stereotype of the capitalist who cannot quit his appointed rounds because of insatiable greed or an atrophied consciousness of the world around him has been prevalent. Goldman does not fit this description. His fascination with business has not stemmed from any desire to accumulate greater wealth but from his satisfaction at using his hard-won skills and knowledge to the fullest extent. When speaking of his latest business venture, the Regency Square project, Goldman makes no reference to the possibilities of profit. He speaks of the unusual beauty of the central fountain plaza, just as in earlier years he felt a thrill at building a larger, more modern supermarket.

That is the way he is—always with a warm feeling for the project of the moment, always with that inner determination that it succeed, whether it is a spectacular fountain or multimillion-dollar business project.

There is much more that could, and perhaps should, be written about Goldman—perhaps an interesting and reflective overview of personality characteristics. For instance, he has a ready sense of humor. A colleague tells a story illustrating Goldman's quick wit: "Near the end of the blisteringly hot picnic-conference, out of the blue came a bird dropping, splashing on the working drawings. In a typical lightning reaction, Syl blurted, 'Just think! For others they sing!'"

Goldman has the courage of his convictions; he can issue immediate orders and never look back. His memory gives him 20-20 hindsight—a kind of clairvoyance that stems from his vast store of experience. Virtually devoid of despair, he has no fear of failure. He is courageous and venturesome. His attitude is compassionate, kindly, happy-go-lucky and bold. To him, today is a joy to be lived to the fullest. He believes that tomorrow does not hold one one-hundredth of the fears conjured up by worry, and so he refuses to be a worrier. Instead he is assertive and positive. His ability to grasp all facets of a problem quickly—to see the broad picture from every perspective—and his unique sense of timing attest to his astuteness. His business acumen is uncanny, his persistence unbelievable. He has a positive "can do" philosophy, and he has the attribute of being able to say no without saying it. He is a determined optimist, always adding something to make a project better. He is helpful to others, sympathetic, colorful, happy, and joyous. His zest for life keeps him youthful and effervescent. To him opportunities abound for everyone. He is the eternal humanitarian.

A dedicated and devoted supporter of his country, Sylvan N. Goldman exemplifies in his behavior the high moral principles on which this nation was founded. As business pioneer, inventor, and philanthropist he has made his state and his nation a better place in which to live. His life has been one of hard work, innovation, and dedication—an inspiration to all Oklahomans.

Notes

CHAPTER 1

1. Sylvan N. Goldman interview, Oklahoma City, February 12, 1974 (hereafter cited as Goldman interview; all interviews utilized in this book were conducted by the author unless otherwise noted).

2. *Ibid.*

3. *Daily Ardmoreite*, November 15, 1898.

4. Mary Evelyn Frost, "The History of Carter County," master's thesis, University of Oklahoma, 1942, pp. 3, 28, 58.

5. *Ibid.*, pp. 30, 58, 61; Paul Nelson Frame, "A History of Ardmore, Oklahoma, from the Earliest Beginnings to 1907," master's thesis, University of Oklahoma, 1949, pp. 32–34, 139.

6. Mrs. Walter Neustadt interview, Ardmore, Oklahoma, April 5, 1974; Goldman interview, February 12, 1974; "Oklahoma Jews," *Encyclopedia Judaica*, Vol. 12, p. 1353; *Daily Ardmoreite*, July 21, 1947.

7. Goldman interview, February 12, 1974.

8. From Mrs. Fred Carr.

9. Goldman interview, February 12, 1974.

10. Harold N. Reed interview, April 20, 1974; William T. Lampe, comp., *Tulsa County in the World War*, pp. 29–30; (hereafter cited as *Tulsa County*).

11. Harold N. Reed Interview, April 20, 1974.

12. Orr C. Riley interview, April 17, 1974.

13. Goldman interview, February 12, 1974.

14. Pierce C. Fredericks, *The Great Adventure: America in the First World War*, p. 49; Lampe, *Tulsa County*, p. 31.

15. *Tulsa Daily World*, January 6, 1919; Goldman interview, February 12, 1974.

16. Fredericks, *The Great Adventure*, pp. 115, 138–39.

17. Harold N. Reed interview, April 20, 1974; Orr C. Riley interview, April 17, 1974.

18. From a letter to Mrs. C. E. Lehman, December 5, 1918, reprinted in *Tulsa Daily World*, January 6, 1919.

19. Goldman interview February 12, 1974; Lampe, *Tulsa County*, pp. 32–33.

20. Fredericks, *The Great Adventure*, pp. 142–46, 156–58.
21. Goldman interview, February 12, 1974.
22. *Daily Oklahoman*, March, 1919.
23. Goldman interview, February 12, 1974.
24. Lampe, *Tulsa County*, pp. 35–37.
25. Goldman interview, February 12, 1974.

CHAPTER 2

1. Goldman interview, February 12, 1974.
2. George Soule, *Prosperity Decade: From War to Depression, 1917–1929*, pp. 95–96.
3. Goldman interview, February 12, 1974.
4. *Ibid.*; Frank J. Charvat, *Supermarketing*, pp. 15–16.
5. Goldman interview, February 12, 1974.
6. *Tulsa Tribune*, April 3, 1927; Goldman interview, February 26, 1974.
7. Arthur S. Link, *American Epoch: A History of the United States since the 1890's*, p. 256.
8. Quoted in Ralph Cassady, Jr., *Competition and Price Making in Food Retailing: The Anatomy of Supermarket Operations*, pp. 3–4.
9. *Ibid.*, pp. 9–10; Charvat, *Supermarketing*, pp. 65–66.
10. "Sylvan N. Goldman," *Oklahoma Publisher*, Vol. 30, No. 3 (May, 1959), p. 12.
11. Goldman interview, February 26, 1974.
12. *Tulsa Tribune*, April 3, 1927.
13. *Ibid.*
14. Goldman interview, February 26, 1974.
15. *Tulsa Tribune*, April 3, 1927.
16. *Ibid.*, December 14, 1928.
17. *Ibid.*, March 3, 1929; Goldman interview, February 26, 1974.
18. For a fuller discussion of margin buying and broker loans as they applied to the 1929 stock market activities, see John Kenneth Galbraith, *The Great Crash, 1929*, pp. 23–27.
19. Goldman interview, February 26, 1974.
20. *Ibid.*

CHAPTER 3

1. According to the census figures for 1929, the stories of ruined speculators leaping from windows constituted a myth. Nevertheless, this image has lingered in the public consciousness as a convenient symbol of the 1929 crash. Galbraith, *The Great Crash, 1929*, pp. 133–37.
2. Goldman interview, February 24, 1974.
3. *Ibid.*, March 5, 1974.

4. *Ibid.*, February 24, 1974.

5. Mrs. Lavinia Morris to Sylvan N. Goldman, Mar. 6, 1930, Goldman Collection, Oklahoma City (all letters cited are in the Goldman Collection unless otherwise noted).

6. Goldman interview, February 24, 1974.

7. Sylvan N. Goldman, "Progress Through Service: A Personal Report to the Employees and Friends of Standard–Humpty Dumpty Super Markets" Oklahoma City, privately printed, 1955, Goldman Collection (hereafter cited as "Progress Through Service").

8. *Sunday Oklahoman, November 21, 1965.*

9. Goldman, "Progress Through Service"; Goldman interview, February 24, 1974.

10. Sylvan N. Goldman, "The Produce Market on a Self-Service Basis: Is It Practical and Profitable?" *Super Market Merchandising*, Vol. 3, No. 10 (October, 1938), pp. 42–43, 85–86 (hereafter cited as "The Produce Market").

11. Goldman, "Progress Through Service."

12. Charvat, *Supermarketing*, pp. 18–19.

13. Joseph Neubauer, "Do Flamboyant Advertising Headlines Pay?" *Super Market Merchandising*, Vol. 3, No. 10 (Oct., 1938), pp. 55–56.

14. See Chapter 5 for a discussion of Goldman's contributions, including the grocery shopping cart.

15. William E. Leuchtenburt, *Franklin D. Roosevelt and the New Deal*, pp. 38–39, 42–44.

16. Goldman interview, March 15, 1974.

17. *Ibid.*, March 25, 1974; handbills published by labor unions, Goldman Collection.

18. Goldman interview, March 25, 1974.

CHAPTER 4

1. Goldman interview, April 20, 1974.

2. These words were spoken during an address to the First Annual Midwest Inventors Conference held in Oklahoma City, quoted in *Oklahoma City Times*, September 28, 1973.

3. Description and specifications are from a Folding Carrier Company advertisement of 1938, Goldman Collection.

4. William H. Marnell, *Once upon a Store: A Biography of the World's First Supermarket*, p. 37.

5. *Ibid.*, pp. 39–40.

6. M. M. Zimmerman, *The Super Market: A Revolution in Distribution*, pp. 27–28.

7. *Oklahoma City Times*, June 4, 1973.

8. *Ibid.*, June 11, 1973.

9. Goldman interview, April 20, 1974.

10. Conway P. Cox to Sylvan N. Goldman, Sept. 9, 1942; Goldman interview, April 20, 1974.

11. Goldman interview, April 20, 1974.

12. The application for a patent was filed April 8, 1939, and granted May 21, 1940. Patent No. 2,201,533, "Store Service Truck," United States Patent Office, Goldman Collection.

13. Jack E. Lurie to Folding Carrier Company, May 31, 1939; W. E. Cook to Folding Carrier Company, August 17, 1939; A. H. Williford to Folding Carrier Company, September 18, 1939; Montgomery Ward to Folding Carrier Company, June 14, 1942.

14. Description from Folding Carrier Company advertisement, 1939, Goldman Collection.

15. "Gerber Baby Food Displays," sales bulletin, Gerber Products Company, Fremont, Michigan, November 13, 1948; "Gerber Display Idea," undated clipping from *Sales Management Magazine*, Goldman Collection.

16. "A Milk Merchandiser for Retail Stores," *Dairy World*, December, 1938, p. 60; "Milk Racks for Use in Display Cases," *Popular Mechanics*, Vol. 106, No. 1 January, 1939), p. 24.

17. Description from Folding Carrier Company advertisements, 1942, 1943, Goldman Collection.

18. R. J. Hogan to Folding Carrier Company, August 22, 1942; I. G. Bentley to A. K. Weiss, December 23, 1940; H. R. Springer to Kurt H. Schweitzer, December 8, 1941.

19. Wallace A. Morse to Folding Carrier Company, January 23, 1942; Ross L. Perryman to Folding Carrier Corporation, August 10, 1942; Lenard H. Campbell, Jr., to Sylvan N. Goldman, January 4, 1946.

20. *Oklahoma City Times*, February 15, 1950.

21. Description from Folding Carrier Company advertisement, 1950, Goldman Collection.

22. *Oklahoma City Times*, July 9, 1942; *Ibid.*, March 10, 1944.

23. *Supermarket News*, September 8, 1852; *Daily Oklahoman*, September 7, 1952; *Southern California Grocers Journal*, October 3, 1952.

24. "Shopping Cart Ads," *Business Week*, February 16, 1974, p. 101.

25. Information from Folding Carrier Company advertisements, 1952, 1954, 1955, Goldman Collection.

26. *Ibid.*

27. Walson et al. v. Heil et al., *U.S. Patent Quarterly*, Vol. 88, pp. 537–38.

28. *Topeka State Journal*, December 22, 1954; *Daily Oklahoman*, July 14, 1956.

29. *Oklahoma City Times*, August 24, 1961; *Sunday Oklahoman*,

August 27, 1972.
  30. *Weekly Turnstile*, July 25, 1938.
  31. Certificate of membership dated February 17, 1939, Goldman Collection.
  32. Undated newspaper clipping, Goldman Collection.
  33. Siphya Store to Folding Carrier Company, April 26, 1952.

CHAPTER 5

1. Goldman, "Progress Through Service."
  2. Description from Folding Carrier Company advertisement, 1944, Goldman Collection.
  3. Goldman, "Progress Through Service."
  4. Charvat, *Supermarketing*, pp. 28–29.
  5. *Ibid.*, pp. 30–46; "The Lush New Suburban Market," *Fortune*, Vol. 48, No. 5 (November, 1953), pp. 131–32.
  6. James R. D. Eddy to Sylvan N. Goldman, July 26, 1949.
  7. Charvat, *Supermarketing*, pp. 228–29; Goldman interview, February 26, 1974.
  8. Goldman, "Progress Through Service."
  9. *Super Marketer*, September 27, 1948; *ibid.*, 1949.
  10. *Ibid.*, November, 1950.
  11. Edward M. Harwell, *Checkout Management*, p. 126.
  12. *Super Marketer*, September, 1951; *ibid.*, December, 1950.
  13. *Daily Ardmoreite*, April 8, 1956.
  14. Zimmerman, *The Super Market*, p. 19.
  15. *Daily Ardmoreite*, April 8, 1956.
  16. *Daily Oklahoman*, March 9, 1945.
  17. Pictures and descriptions of these promotional materials are in Goldman Collection.
  18. *Daily Oklahoman*, August 3, 1958; *Oklahoma City Britton North Star*, September 18, 1958.
  19. Charvat, *Supermarketing*, pp. 168–69.
  20. Goldman, "Progress Through Service"; *Sunday Oklahoman*, Nov. 12, 1967.
  21. "Behind ACF-Brill's Big Switch," Business Week, May 19, 1956, pp. 195–97; "Report on ACF-Wrigley Stores, Inc., *et al.*," Dun & Bradstreet, Inc., January 23, 1956, Goldman Collection.
  22. "Agreement of Merger, dated November 1, 1957 . . . ," Goldman Collection.
  23. *Ibid.*; "Behind ACF-Brill's Big Switch," *Business Week*; Goldman interview, April 22, 1974.
  24. Goldman interview, April 22, 1974.

CHAPTER 6

1. M. M. Zimmerman, *The Challenge of Chain Stores Distribution.*
2. Zimmerman, *The Super Market*, pp. 73–76.
3. Picture and description of exhibit in Goldman Collection.
4. Zimmerman, *The Super Market*, pp. 82–83.
5. Sylvan N. Goldman, "Produce on Self-Service Basis," *Executive Service on Food Distribution*, No. 250 (1938), p. 9. For a brief discussion of the article see Chapter 3.
6. M. M. Zimmerman to Sylvan N. Goldman, July 24, 1939, Goldman Collection.
7. Quoted in Zimmerman, *The Super Market*, pp. 87–88.
8. "Convention Panelists Speak Out," *Super Market Merchandising*, Vol. 4, No. 10 (October, 1939), p. 27.
9. Sylvan N. Goldman, "The Outlook for Super Market Expansion During the Coming Year," *Super Market Merchandising*, Vol. 5, No. 10 (October, 1940), pp. 12, 36–37.
10. *New York Times*, September 21, 1943; Zimmerman, *The Super Market*, pp. 88–89.
11. Leo W. Smith to Sylvan N. Goldman, January 13, 1943, Goldman Collection.
12. "Conference Attracts Nation-Wide Attendance," *Super Market Merchandising*, Vol. 9, No. 7 (July, 1944), p. 15.
13. Zimmerman, *The Super Market*, p. 95.
14. *Oklahoma City Times*, August 3, 1948.
15. Don Parsons to Sylvan N. Goldman, April 30, 1949, Goldman Collection; *SMI Carrier*, December 1949, p. 1.
16. *SMI Carrier*, October, 1949; *Super Marketer*, April 1951.
17. *Super Marketer*, June, 1951; *New York Journal of Commerce*, May 17, 1951.
18. Goldman Collection.
19. *SMI Carrier*, pp. 7–8; *Super Marketer*, September 1951; *New York Journal of Commerce*, September 7, 1951.
20. *Super Marketer*, March, 1951; SMI Information Service Bulletin 21, Goldman Collection.
21. Goldman Collection.
22. *SMI Carrier*, May, 1953.
23. *Cleveland Press*, May 15, 1952.
24. Copy of the resolution of May 15, 1952, Goldman Collection.
25. *New York Journal of Commerce*, May 20, 1952.
26. *Utica Press*, May 17, 1952.
27. "The Super Market Industry Speaks: A Factual Report by the Members of Super Market Institute," pp. 10–12, Goldman Collection.
28. Goldman interview, April 20, 1974. This estimation of the food

industry holds true today. Gordon F. Bloom, of Massachusetts Institute of Technology, told an interviewer in May, 1974, that "the era of cheap food in America is at an end." He blamed the increased labor costs for the high prices of the 1960's. He indicated that the way to eliminate runaway overhead expenses was through a streamlining effort by the industry to remove all inefficiencies in packaging and shipping. He also urged innovative cost-saving ideas such as use of lasers or sonic beams to cut meat. *Daily Oklahoman*, May 21, 1974.

29. *SMI Carrier*, January, 1952.
30. Goldman Collection.
31. *SMI Carrier*, December, 1951.
32. Goldman Collection.
33. *Ibid*.
34. Zimmerman, *The Super Market*, p. 117.
35. Sylvan N. Goldman, "How Cooperation Can Produce 'More for all,'" *Food Field Reporter*, July 30, 1951, p. 2.
36. Goldman Collection; Zimmerman, *The Super Market*, p. 101.
37. John A. Logan to Sylvan N. Goldman, October 31, 1946, Goldman Collection.
38. Wallace N. Flint to Sylvan N. Goldman, October 26, 1956, August 20, 1958, Goldman Collection.
39. *Super Marketer*, June 18, 1953; *Supermarket News*, June 22, 1953.
40. *Oklahoma City Britton North Star*, undated clipping, Goldman Collection.
41. Zimmerman, *The Super Market*, pp. 294–97.

CHAPTER 7

1. Robert A. Magowan to Sylvan N. Goldman, January 15, 1960, Goldman Collection.
2. *Fort Worth Star-Telegram*, January 3, 1952.
3. Goldman interview, April 20, 1974.
4. Jo Davidson, *Between Sittings: An Informal Autobiography*, pp. 298–299.
5. *Ibid.*, pp. 299–300.
6. Taken from one of the invitations, Goldman Collection.
7. Resolution from the Board of Directors, Oklahoma City Chamber of Commerce to Sylvan N. Goldman, January 3, 1952, Goldman Collection.
8. *Oklahoma City Times*, January 9, 1952.
9. *Daily Oklahoman*, December 16, 1960; Goldman interview, April 20, 1974.
10. *Tulsa Daily World*, June 11, 1953.
11. *Ibid.*, January 28, 1954.

12. *Ibid.*, June 4, 1954; *ibid.*, January 14, 1955.
13. *Oklahoma City Times*, January 31, 1960.
14. *Ibid.*, September 24, 1962.
15. *Ibid.*, October 18, 1961; *Tulsa Daily World*, February 18, 1962.
16. *Tulsa Daily World*, December 16, 1964; Sylvan N. Goldman to Dean Krakel, November 3, 1972; Richard Muno to Sylvan N. Goldman, July 12, 1972; Dean Krakel to Sylvan N. Goldman, July 15, 1972, Goldman Collection.
17. Leonard McMurray interview, Norman, Oklahoma, March 13, 1974.
18. *Ibid.*
19. *Ibid.*; *Daily Oklahoman*, October 27, 1961.
20. *Ibid.*
21. Glenn Snider interview, Norman, Oklahoma, March 13, 1974.
22. Oklahoma Center for Continuing Education, *The Southwest Center for Human Relations Studies* (Norman, 1973), pp. 4–5, Goldman collection.
23. Sylvan N. Goldman, "Memorandum Regarding the Human Relations Center and the Goldman Chain" (undated manuscript); George Henderson to Sylvan N. Goldman, May 20, 1971; Sylvan N. Goldman to Peter Kyle McCarter, September 23, 1970, Goldman collection.
24. Ibid., pp. 9–11; Oklahoma Center for Continuing Education, *Annual Report of the Southwest Center for Human Relations Studies, 1969*, pp. 3–4, 7–9, 11, Goldman Collection.
25. *Sunday Oklahoman*, August 9, 1970.
26. Jack Durland, "Oklahoma Hall of Fame Citation for Mr. Sylvan N. Goldman, November 16, 1971," pp. 3–5, Goldman Collection.

CHAPTER 8

1. The material in this chapter is extracted from interviews by the author with Sylvan N. Goldman and his family.

CHAPTER 9

1. H. Arthur Littell interview, Oklahoma City, May 7, 1974.
2. *Ibid.*
3. Goldman interview, April 20, 1974.
4. *Ibid.*
5. *Oklahoma City Times*, July 7, 1974.
6. Goldman interview, April 20, 1974.
7. *Ibid.*
8. *Oklahoma City Times*, February 25, 1966; *Wall Street Journal*, February 25, 1966.
9. Goldman interview, April 20, 1974.

10. *Daily Oklahoman*, April 15, 1955; *ibid.*, April 20, 1955.
11. *Oklahoma City Times*, April 27, 1955; *Capital Hill Beacon*, October 16, 1955.
12. Goldman interview, April 20, 1974.
13. Otero Savings, "Statement of Conditions," June 30, 1978; *Otero Club Newsletter*, January, 1974, Goldman Collection.
14. H. Arthur Littell interview, Oklahoma City, April 20, 1974.
15. Peter Boatright interview, Oklahoma City, May 7, 1974.

Bibliography

PRIVATE COLLECTIONS

Sylvan N. Goldman Collection, Oklahoma City.

GOVERNMENT DOCUMENTS

The U.S. Patent Quarterly. Vol. 88. Washington, D.C.: U.S. Government Printing Office, 1961.

INTERVIEWS

Peter Boatright, Oklahoma City, May 7, 1975.
Mrs. Fred Carr, Ardmore, Oklahoma, March 29, 1974.
Monte and Alfred Goldman, Oklahoma City, March 7, 1974.
Sylvan N. Goldman, Oklahoma City, February 12, 24, 26, March 5, 15, 25, April 20, 22, 1974.
H. Arthur Littell, Oklahoma City, March 7, May 7, 1974.
Leonard McMurray, Oklahoma City, May 29, 1974.
Mrs. Walter Neustadt, Ardmore, Oklahoma, April 5, 1974.
Harold N. Reed, Oklahoma City, April 20, 1974.
Orr C. Riley, Tulsa, Oklahoma, April 17, 1974.
Glenn Snider, Norman, Oklahoma, March 13, 1974.
Typescript of Charles Kuralt Interview with Sylvan N. Goldman, Oklahoma City, for "Who's Who."

NEWSPAPERS

Capital Hill Beacon (Oklahoma City)
Cleveland Press
Daily Ardmoreite
Daily and Sunday Oklahoman
Houston Post
New York Journal of Commerce
New York Times

Oklahoma Journal
Oklahoma City, Britton North Star
Oklahoma City Times
SMI Carrier
Southern California Grocers Journal
Southwest Jewish Chronicle
Star-Telegram (Fort Worth)
Super Market News
Super Marketer
Topeka State Journal
Tulsa Daily World
Tulsa Tribune
Utica (New York) *Press*
Wall Street Journal
Weekly Turnstile

THESES

Frame, Paul Nelson. "A History of Ardmore, Oklahoma, from the Earliest Beginnings to 1907," master's thesis, University of Oklahoma, 1949.
Frost, Mary Evelyn. "The History of Carter County," master's thesis, University of Oklahoma, 1942.

BOOKS

Bremner, Robert H. *American Philanthropy.* Chicago, University of Chicago Press, 1960.
Bloomfield, Daniel, ed. *Chain Stores and Legislation.* New York, H. W. Wilson Company, 1939.
Cassady, Ralph, Jr. *Competition and Price Making in Food Retailing: The Anatomy of Supermarket Operations.* New York, Ronald Press Co., 1962.
Charvat, Frank J. *Supermarketing.* New York, Macmillan Company, 1961.
Davidson, Jo. *Between Sittings: An Informal Autobiography.* New York, Dial Press, 1951.
Fredericks, Pierce G. *The Great Adventure: America in the First World War.* New York, E. P. Dutton & Co., 1960.

Galbraith, John Kenneth. *The Great Crash, 1929.* Boston, Houghton Mifflin Company, 1961.

Glazer, Nathan. *American Judaism.* 2d ed., rev. Chicago, University of Chicago Press, 1972.

Harwell, Edward M. *Checkout Management.* New York, Chain Store Publishing Corporation, 1963.

Jones, Maldwyn Allen. *American Immigration.* Chicago, University of Chicago Press, 1960.

Karp, Abraham J., ed. *The Jewish Experience in America: Selected Studies from the Publications of the American Jewish Historical Society.* New York, KTAV Publishing House, Inc. 1969.

Lampe, William T., comp. *Tulsa County in the World War.* Tulsa, Triangle Printing Co., 1919.

Lebhar, Godfrey M. *Chain Stores in America, 1859–1950.* New York, Chain Store Publishing Corporation, 1952.

Leuchtenburg, William E. *Franklin D. Roosevelt and the New Deal, 1932–1940.* New York, Harper & Row, 1963.

Link, Arthur S. *American Epoch: A History of the United States Since the 1890's,* 2d ed., rev. New York, Alfred A. Knopf, 1965.

Lundberg, Ferdinand. *The Rich and the Super-Rich: A Study in the Power of Money Today.* New York, Lyle Stuart, Inc., 1968.

Marnell, William H. *Once Upon a Store: A Biography of the World's First Supermarket.* New York, Herder and Herder, 1971.

Soule, George. *Prosperity Decade: from War to Depression, 1917–1929.* New York, Holt, Rinehart & Winston, 1947.

Yaffe, James. *The American Jews.* New York, Random House, 1968.

Zimmerman, M. M. *The Challenge of Chain Stores Distribution.*
———. *The Super Market: A Revolution in Distribution.* New York, McGraw-Hill Book Co., Inc., 1955.

ARTICLES

"Behind ACF-Brill's Big Switch," *Business Week,* May 19, 1956, pp. 195–97.

"Conference Attracts Nation-Wide Attendance," *Super Market*

Merchandising, Vol. LX, No. 7 (July, 1944), pp. 15–17.

Goldman, Sylvan N. "How Cooperation Can Produce 'More for All,'" *Food Field Reporter*, July 30, 1951, p. 2.

_____. "The Outlook for Super Market Expansion During the Coming Year," *Super Market Merchandising*, Vol. 5, No. 10 (October, 1940), pp. 12, 36–37.

_____. "The Produce Department on a Self-Service Basis: Is it Practical and Profitable?" *Super Market Merchandising*, Vol. III, No. 10 (October, 1938), pp. 42–43, 85–86.

_____ "Produce on Self-Service Basis," *Executive Service on Food Distribution*, No. 250 (1938), pp. 9–11.

_____. "Progress Through Service: A Personal Report to the Employees and Friends of Standard–Humpty Dumpty Super Markets," Oklahoma City, privately printed, 1955.

"The Lush New Suburban Market," *Fortune*, Vol. XLVIII, No. 5 (November, 1953), pp. 131–133.

"A Milk Merchandiser for Retail Stores," *Dairy World*, December, 1938, p. 60.

"Milk Racks for Use in Display Cases," *Popular Mechanics*, Vol. 106 (January, 1939), p. 24.

Neubauver, Joseph. "Do Flamboyant Advertising Headlines Pay?" *Super Market Merchandising*. Vol. III, No. 10 (October, 1938), pp. 55–58.

"Shopping Cart Aids," *Business Week*, February 16, 1974, p. 101.

Index